Dedication

In memory of my beloved mother,

Sylvia (Zilla bas Davied) ע״ה

whose faith and devotion continue to guide me.

In honor of my father Benno (Binyamin Zev ben Rabbi Dovied Zwi) שליט״א who taught me perseverance, strength, and creativity

With deep appreciation and respect to my teacher,

Rabbi Itsche Rosenbaum and Rebbetzin Chanie Rosenbaum שליט״א

a shining example of Torah and chessed — living proof that kindness must be done regardless of their own situation, uplifting all who cross their path.

With gratitude and esteem Rabbi and Mrs. Nechemya Ort and the chabura.

for their encouragement, inspiration, and acts of kindness that continue to uplift all who are learning with me, the chavrusa shaft, the comradery and together plowing shas.

Closing Blessing:

May these words of Musar and emunah be an elevation for the neshamos of my forebears, and a source of blessing, health, and light for those honored here in life.

Who This Book Is For

This sefer is for parents whose hearts are full of love and questions—mothers and fathers who yearn to return to Hashem and to bring their adult children with them, not by pressure but by presence. It is for families who have traveled different roads and now wish to walk together again; for homes where faith once felt natural and for homes where faith was complicated; for those who kept every Shabbos and those who are learning to light one candle again.

It is for the father who wonders how to speak without lecturing, the mother who longs to invite without insisting, and the son or daughter who wants to be respected as an adult while being welcomed as a child. It is for grandparents who dream of blessing little hands, for newlyweds balancing work and mitzvos, and for anyone who needs words that heal rather than win.

You will find here sources from Chazal, clear guidance for real-life conversations, small practices you can begin today, and stories that honor the dignity of every soul. If you are ready to rebuild trust—with Hashem, with yourself, and with one another—may these pages be a gentle companion on the road home. May the Ribbono Shel Olam meet you at every step.

Table of Contents

The speech that was not given.	8
The Check That Did Not Bounce	12
The Contract That Remained Unsigned	16
The Fence That Disappeared	21
The Exam That Defined Him	26
The Song in the Hospital Room	31
The Broken Pitcher: Gratitude in Loss (הכרת הטוב)	35
The Rabbi and the Thief: Patience That Transforms (סבלנות)	43
The Candle of Forgiveness: Lighting the Darkness (מחילה)	48
The Silent Victory: Mastering the Self (כיבוש היצר)	52
The Weight of a Single Word: The Power of Speech (שמירת הלשון)	57
The Lost Purse: Honesty Beyond Trial (יֹשֶׁר)	61
The Coat on the Road: Boundless Chesed (חסד)	65
The Broken Chair: Humility in Honor (ענווה)	69
The Widow's Bread: Gratitude in Poverty	73
The Empty Seat: Compassion Above Anger (רחמים)	76
The Rain That Never Came: Faith in the Dry Season (אמונה)	80
The Closed Shop: Faith and Shabbos	84
The Physician's Hands: Emunah in Illness (אמונה בחולי)	87
The Empty Cradle: Faith Through Tears (אמונה)..	90
The Last Coin: Faith in Livelihood (אמונה בפרנסה)	93
The Road to Nowhere: Faith in Exile (אמונה בגלות)	96
The Bridge of Faith: Crossing Over (אמונה במעבר)	99
The Soldier's Psalm: Faith in Danger (אמונה בסכנה)	105
The Lone Soldier — The Sacrifice of Arrelle	119
In Six Days the World Changed Forever	112
The Yeshiva in Crisis	128
The Candle in the Storm: Holding Fast to Faith (אמונה)	131

The Yom Kippur War 134
About the Author 152

COPYRIGHT PAGE

Title: *Rediscovering Emuna*
Subtitle: *Coming Home to Hashem—Finding Our Way Back to Serving Him Wholeheartedly, in This World*
Author: Rabbi Dovied Zwi van der Velde
Publisher: Home Safe Home Inc.

Copyright © 2025 by Rabbi Dovied Zwi van der Velde. All rights reserved. This publication is protected by U.S. and international copyright laws. No part of this book may be reproduced, stored in a retrieval system, shared, resold, or transmitted in any form or by any means—electronic, mechanical, photocopying, recording, scanning, or otherwise—without prior written permission and/or a paid license from the publisher, except for brief quotations in reviews permitted by law.

Commercial use & licensing: To request print, digital, coursepack, translation, audio, performance, classroom, or excerpt permissions, contact:
Rights & Permissions — Home Safe Home Inc.
72 Foxwood Rd, Lakewood, NJ 08701, USA
Tel: +1 (917) 681-5189 • Email: HomeSafeHome613@gmail.com

Anti-piracy notice: Unauthorized copying, distribution, or uploading of this work (including to file-sharing sites) is illegal and strictly prohibited. Infringers may be subject to civil and criminal penalties.

Scripture/quotation credits (if applicable):
Scripture quotations are from [translation/edition], used by permission. Additional third-party excerpts appear by permission of their respective rights holders.

Disclaimer: This work presents faith-based teaching and inspiration. Illustrative stories may be adapted or composited to protect privacy; any resemblance to actual persons or events is coincidental unless stated. The author and publisher have made every effort to ensure accuracy; any errors or omissions are unintentional.

Trademarks: Product and company names mentioned are trademarks of their respective owners; use is for identification only and does not imply endorsement.

ISBN (print): 979-8-9997650-1-7
ISBN (eBook): [TBD]
Library of Congress Control Number: [If available]

Cover design: D. Z. van der Velde
Interior design/typesetting: Home Safe Home Inc.
Proofreading: Many wonderful individuals—thank you all!

Printed in the United States of America.
10 9 8 7 6 5 4 3 2 1
First Edition: October 2025

The Speech That Wasn't Given

"The reward of humility is fear of Hashem, riches, honor, and life." (Mishlei 22:4)

When the new synagogue on Cedar Lane was completed, the community decided to hold a grand dedication. The ark doors gleamed with walnut polish, and the letters of *Shema Yisrael* shone in polished brass. Folding chairs were lined up in neat rows, and the air already carried the smell of kugel waiting in the hall.

For nearly a month the committee had argued about who should speak first. Finally, they agreed on Rabbi Meir—the one who had carried the entire responsibility: running the fundraising, overseeing the builder, and calming every storm along the way.

He had carefully prepared his words: how a synagogue is more than stone, how each donation is a block in eternity, how the Shechinah itself would dwell here. Into his notes he had placed a verse from Tehillim and stories from his Rebbe.

On the morning of the dedication, he put on his best hat, kissed his children, and set out for Cedar Lane. Neighbors greeted him with smiles: "Rabbi, today is your day!" Each word added a small stone to the pile of pride in his heart. He told himself: perhaps this is no sin at all—after all, he had given years of labor to build this house.

The Disappointment

Moments before the program began, the chairman came over and whispered:
 "Rabbi Meir, we thought it would be fitting if the mayor spoke first—to honor the city, a bit of political respect. Only five minutes."

Rabbi Meir nodded, though something sharp pricked his heart. The mayor? A man who barely set foot in synagogue, except when the cameras flashed? To place him before words of Torah and thanks to the Master of the Universe?

He reasoned: it's only five minutes.

But the mayor spoke for twenty. About "cultural centers," "community partnerships," and even about "property values." The people clapped politely. Rabbi Meir felt a stone pressing on his chest.

Then the chairman stood again:
 "And now, before our dear Rabbi speaks, let us call up our beloved patron, Mr. Levin, whose generosity made this house possible."

Applause thundered. Mr. Levin, tall and steady, came up to the podium. He spoke about heritage, about family, about building for generations. He shared contractor anecdotes and jokes that landed well. The hall laughed.

When he finally finished, the room buzzed with energy. The chairman leaned toward Rabbi Meir:
 "So sorry—we've run out of time before Minchah. You'll speak after prayers, at the meal."

The Choice

The Rabbi sat, his sermon folded in his pocket, his heart pounding. He could break through. He could rise and declare: "A moment—before Minchah, we must hear Torah." Likely no one would stop him.

But then he noticed something else.

In the back row sat a boy of about thirteen, eyes wide, hands clasped. His lips moved quietly, as though repeating something. Then the chairman called his name: "Moshe'le, go lead *Ashrei*."

The boy stood, trembling, and for the first time in his life led the congregation in prayer. His voice cracked once, then grew stronger, and the room filled with an innocent melody. People encouraged him. His father wept with joy.

And Rabbi Meir understood.

This was not his stage. The honor belonged to Hashem. And today that honor was expressed in a boy's first *Ashrei*.

He let the thought settle. He remained silent, answering prayers with intent. His sermon stayed in his pocket like a letter one chooses not to send.

Afterward

At the meal someone asked him to say a few words. Rabbi Meir rose and spoke briefly:

"Friends, we have built walls, but it is your prayers that will make this a home for the Shechinah. Today, when the young man led *Ashrei*, I believed the foundations of this synagogue truly took root."

A silence fell, deeper than applause. And in that silence, the Rabbi felt something higher than honor. He felt freedom.

Lesson

Sometimes the greatest honor does not come from taking the podium, but from stepping back and letting others shine. Our sages teach: *"He who flees from honor, honor pursues him."*

That evening, Rabbi Meir went home without ever giving his sermon—

but with a heart full of peace.

The Check That Didn't Bounce

"הַבּוֹטֵחַ בַּה' חֶסֶד יְסוֹבְבֶנּוּ."

"Whoever trusts in Hashem will be surrounded by kindness." (Tehillim 32:10)

The Struggle

Moshe Klein sat at his kitchen table in Boro Park. The light above him hummed softly while a stack of unpaid bills stretched out before him like hostile troops. In two days the rent was due. Letters from three different yeshivos—each a tuition reminder—were bundled together in a threatening pile. On top lay the envelope from the electric company, stamped in red: **Final Notice**.

He rubbed his forehead and whispered,
—Ribono Shel Olam, I don't know how to keep this up anymore.

For months his small hardware store had been bleeding out. First the big chains moved into the neighborhood, then a storm flooded his basement inventory. The insurance paid out hardly anything. Every night he went to bed with numbers grinding in his head; every morning he woke to the same knot in his stomach.

That night was worse. He had just written a check to his landlord knowing there wasn't enough in the account to cover it. Unless a miracle happened, the check would bounce—and with it, the last shred of his dignity.

The Despair

His wife, Rivka, slipped quietly into the kitchen and set a steaming cup of tea by his elbow.
—Moshe, she said gently, you always tell the children: *Gam zu l'tovah*—this too is for the good. Do you still believe it?

He wanted to nod, but instead he hid his face in his hands.
—I believe it, but I don't see it. I feel like I'm letting everyone down.

She squeezed his shoulder in encouragement.
—You're not letting anyone down. You're being tested. That's something very different.

After she went to bed, Moshe sat at the table a long time. The clock ticked past midnight. Around one o'clock he opened his Tehillim. His eyes fell on the verse: **"השלך על ה' יהבך והוא יכלכלך"**—"Cast your burden upon Hashem, and He will sustain you." He read it again and again until the words turned from ink into balm on his heart.

He whispered,
—Hashem, I don't see any models that add up, no numbers that work. But I'm placing the burden in Your hands. If You want me to survive, I will. And if not, I will still call You good.

With that surrender, he finally closed his eyes.

The Turning Point

The next morning he dragged himself to the store. The shelves looked bare, the walls gray. He stacked boxes of nails just to look busy. At ten o'clock a tall man in a suit walked in, a folder under his arm.

—Are you Moshe Klein?

Moshe stiffened.
—Yes.

The man smiled kindly.
—I'm with a construction company up north. We're renovating an old boarding school. We need large quantities of hardware: hinges, locks, screws, paint supplies. Your name was given to us by someone who said you're honest.

Moshe blinked in disbelief.
—Bulk...?

The man flipped through the papers in his folder.
—We'd like to open an account today. The estimate is thirty thousand dollars.

Moshe's knees nearly gave way. He stammered,
—We... we can make that happen.

That very afternoon the order was placed and the deposit transferred. Moshe called the bank at once: the check to the landlord would clear. And not only that—the electric bill too.

The Aftermath

That evening Moshe stood at the same kitchen table. The bills were still there, but now, among them, lay a deposit slip—a small banner of hope. He took Rivka's hand and whispered,

—You were right. The test wasn't about the numbers, but about holding on until the light broke through.

Rivka smiled.

—It's always darkest right before *Shacharis*.

Reflection

Despair is seductive. It whispers that we are alone, abandoned. But *emunah* isn't about seeing the rescue in advance; it's about trusting that the One who has carried you until now won't drop you now.

The check didn't bounce—not because the numbers magically changed, but because Hashem already had a plan in place, waiting for the moment Moshe chose trust over despair.

Source Note

Hebrew:
"הַבּוֹטֵחַ בַּה' חֶסֶד יְסוֹבְבֶנּוּ." (Tehillim 32:10)

Translation:
"Whoever trusts in Hashem will be surrounded by kindness." (Tehillim 32:10)

The Contract Left Unsigned

"Who is rich? He who rejoices in his portion." (Pirkei Avot 4:1)

The Setting

The late afternoon light of lower Manhattan streamed through glass walls, gilding the skyline with a deceptive warmth. Inside the corner office, silence hung thick, broken only by the faint hum of the city far below. Avi Rosen sat hunched over an expanse of polished mahogany, his reflection mingling with the shimmer of a document that promised more than it had any right to promise.

The contract glared up at him — pages that spoke of prosperity, of debts erased, of security at last. All that was required was his name, a stroke of ink, a surrender written in neat cursive.

Across the table lounged the other man: well-tailored, cufflinks catching the light, a smile crafted with the ease of one accustomed to closing deals. His voice, smooth as oiled leather, slid into the stillness.

"It is very simple, Avi. You source. I distribute. We split the profits. Fifty–fifty. Nothing more complicated than that."

On the page, the numbers glittered like jewels. A single flourish of his pen, and tuition fees would vanish, the mortgage would no longer shadow their meals, and Rivky would not whisper anxiously about groceries each Friday. The arithmetic of relief was intoxicating.

Yet beneath the table Avi's stomach twisted. He knew this man — not from the synagogue, not from circles of upright commerce. There were whispers: shipments that skirted the law's edge, invoices that shifted like sand, cargo that passed through customs wrapped in ambiguity. No charge had ever been proved, nothing written that could be prosecuted — but the stench of smoke clung all the same.

The Battle Within

Think of the freedom, he told himself. *Think of Rivky's smile when the debts are gone. Think of the children's shoes, unscuffed by worry. Think of peace at last.*

But a counter-voice pressed harder, stern and insistent: *Wealth born of shadows brings those very shadows into one's home. The meal you serve will be seasoned with unease. The walls you strengthen will tremble with shame.*

He remembered his rebbi's words, spoken years earlier with the weight of prophecy: "A deal that costs your honesty or your shalom is not profit — it is poison. It will curdle in your hands."

The man across the table nudged the contract closer, his cufflinks flashing like bait. "Sign today. The first shipment leaves Monday. Don't overthink it, Avi. Everyone does it this way. Only a fool asks too many questions."

Avi's hand hovered above the pen. The weight of the office pressed upon him. The city's skyline, glittering through the glass, seemed to lean forward, daring him to choose.

The Turning Point

And then — unbidden — an image rose in his mind: his home after bedtime, the quiet breathing of his children, their faces luminous with innocence in the half-light. He imagined himself entering their rooms, tucking blankets beneath their chins, and knowing that the food upon their table had been purchased with dishonor. Would he be able to look into their eyes — those clear, unclouded eyes — and say, *"Abba did this for you"*?

The thought scorched him. His hand trembled more violently. And then, slowly, deliberately, he placed the pen down upon the table.

"I cannot," he said. The words fell into the room like stones into water, rippling against the slick surface of the man's composure.

The smile on the other's lips faltered, hardened into disdain. "You'll regret this. Opportunities like this do not come twice. Men who refuse me often find themselves wishing they had chosen differently."

Avi stood, heart hammering, the tremor in his knees betrayed only to himself. "Perhaps. But I would rather regret losing money than regret losing myself."

He left the office with empty pockets — yet the air felt cleaner as the door shut behind him.

The Aftermath

The weeks that followed tested every sinew of his resolve. Money was scarce, thinner than ever. Avi took on odd jobs, delivered merchandise personally, shouldered burdens that bent his back but not his spirit. At night he and Rivky sat together at the worn kitchen table, reviewing expenses with ruthless precision, pruning every unnecessary branch. It was not ease — but it was peace. There was laughter at supper, warmth between them, a gentleness born of shared trial.

Months passed. Then one morning, as ordinary as any other, a new client appeared. A large distributor, reputable and established, sought him out. "Your name came to me," the man said, "with one word attached — honesty. We prefer suppliers we can trust."

Orders multiplied. Growth came not in a sudden flood of fortune, but in a steady river of clean, transparent trade. Slowly, brick by brick, a foundation of integrity bore fruit.

One evening, while tucking his youngest child into bed, the boy asked with the artless candor of children:
 "Abba, are we rich?"

Avi smiled, his heart soft with gratitude.
 "Yes, baruch Hashem. We have what we need."

And in that quiet moment he felt, not as theory but as truth, the wisdom of the Mishnah: wealth is not measured in possessions amassed, but in a soul at peace with its portion.

Reflection

Greed is a seductive whisper, promising that just a little more will mend every fracture. Yet contentment replies with a deeper music: *what you already hold is blessing enough*.

True wealth lies not in the abundance of one's accounts, but in the clear conscience that allows a father to meet his children's gaze unflinching, and a husband to clasp his wife's hand without shame.

And so the contract remained unsigned — the fortune untaken, the poison refused. What Avi gained was not the fleeting comfort of numbers on a page, but the enduring wealth of integrity, of a heart that can rest untroubled beneath the gaze of Heaven.

The Fence That Disappeared

"Seek peace and pursue it." (Tehillim 34:15)

The Encroachment

For more than two decades, the quiet street in Passaic had been defined by its unchanging rhythms: children bicycling in the evenings, the faint fragrance of challah drifting from kitchen windows on Fridays, and the steadfast presence of two neighbors who, though not intimate friends, had lived side by side in amicable silence.

Mr. Friedman, a retired rebbi, cultivated roses along the narrow strip that bordered his property. He trimmed them with almost priestly care, watering them in the early morning when the dew was still heavy, whispering berachos under his breath as though each bud was an emissary of divine beauty.

Next door stood the Adler home. Younger, prosperous, brimming with activity. Recently, Adler had undertaken a major renovation of his backyard: a broad wooden deck, a bright swing set for his children, and finally, the crowning symbol of privacy — a tall wooden fence.

At first, Friedman hardly noticed. The fence was new, neat, and unassuming. But one day, as he bent over to cut away withered branches from his roses, his eye caught the surveyor's stone near the corner of his yard. The fence did not align with it. It pressed inward. A sliver of his land — modest but real — had been swallowed.

Something in his chest tightened.

The Fire Within

His children, upon hearing of it, erupted with indignation.
"Tatty, you cannot ignore this. It's your land. Call a surveyor, take it to a din Torah. Why should you be cheated?"

Their words stoked the ember already smoldering within him. It wasn't simply earth or boundary; it was two decades of care, of responsibility, of an unspoken covenant between man and soil. He had preserved what was his. And now? A neighbor had, with a shrug of wood and nails, claimed it as his own.

That Shabbos, Friedman found himself restless, unable to enter fully into prayer. The siddur lay open before him, yet his thoughts marched elsewhere — to imagined confrontations. He saw himself presenting proof, unrolling maps, demanding justice. He saw the fence toppled, his roses stretching unbound toward the sun.

And yet... when the congregation reached *Oseh Shalom*, the words seemed to pierce through his storm: *"He Who makes peace in His heavens, may He make peace upon us."* A whisper of conscience rose: *Peace is not secured in courts; it is grown, like roses, through patience and humility.*

He recalled his rebbi's voice from years long past: *"The ground you surrender for the sake of shalom may one day become the ground upon which your portion in Olam Haba stands."*

Still, the question tormented him: was he strong enough to let go?

The Knock at the Door

Sunday afternoon, Friedman's resolve crystallized. He walked across the narrow stretch of lawn, his steps steady though his heart thundered. He knocked.

Adler opened the door, shoulders squared, eyes guarded — a man bracing himself for battle.

But what he encountered was not anger. Friedman's lined face bore only a gentle smile.

"I noticed," said Friedman quietly, "that the new fence cuts a little into my property. Perhaps by right it belongs to me. But listen… if it makes your yard safer for your children, let it remain. I have roses enough on my side."

For a moment, Adler only stared, suspicion flickering across his features. Then incredulity.
 "You're serious? You won't bring this to a rav? You won't contest it?"

Friedman shook his head.
 "Better we remain neighbors than adversaries. I want our children to greet each other on Shabbos, not to avert their eyes."

Shame crept over Adler's face, flushing it crimson. His voice faltered.
 "Reb Friedman… I never meant to wrong you. The contractor must have misread the map. I'll move it back. Tomorrow."

But Friedman lifted his hand in a gesture of dismissal. "No need. Leave it as it is. What matters most is shalom."

The Harvest of Peace

A week later, Adler arrived at Friedman's door, his children in tow, holding a tray of cake. His words stumbled.
"For Shabbos... and... thank you."

Over the months that followed, something invisible yet unmistakable blossomed between the two families. The children played across the fence line, their laughter bridging wood and soil. A ball forgotten on one side was tossed back without hesitation. Even Friedman's roses seemed to lean against the fence with quiet companionship, as though sanctifying the wood that once symbolized conflict.

Years passed. When at last Reb Friedman departed this world, Adler stood at his funeral, tears streaking his cheeks. His sons watched as he whispered, "He taught me the meaning of peace. He showed me that losing land is nothing compared to gaining a neighbor."

Reflection

Strife diminishes worlds. Peace enlarges them. At times, peace is not achieved through negotiation or compromise but through surrender — through relinquishing what is "rightfully mine" in pursuit of what is eternally right.

Source:

"בקש שלום ורדפהו." (Tehillim 34:15)

"Seek peace and pursue it."

The Exam That Defined Him

"Lying lips are an abomination to Hashem."
(Mishlei 12:22)

The Setup

The campus library on finals week was less a sanctuary of learning than a battlefield of nerves. Pencils clicked like restless metronomes, keyboards rattled like nervous teeth, and the stale odor of over-brewed coffee hung in the air like a second ceiling.

At one table, half hidden beneath a tower of textbooks and graphs, sat David Stein. His shirt collar was open, his eyes rimmed red from nights of relentless study, and his fingers dug into his temples as though he could squeeze formulas into permanence by force of will. Tomorrow's economics exam would decide everything — not merely a grade, but his scholarship, his fragile foothold in the world of academia, his ability to remain in school at all.

Without it, there was nothing. No tuition, no books, no hope of finishing the degree that had already cost him so many sleepless nights. His wife, visibly pregnant, had asked him that morning if they would manage the hospital bills. He had smiled, but the smile had been a paper-thin mask stretched over the panic inside.

And then — the phone. A small vibration against the table. He turned it over.

A message glowed on the screen:

"I have the test questions. Got them from a friend in admin. Want them?"

David's pulse surged. The words were short, casual, but they thundered in his chest. He had studied, yes. But he knew this professor: merciless, surgical in his cruelty, designing exams that stripped away any illusion of preparedness.

This — this was salvation offered in pixels. His wife's calm. His father's approval. His child's future. All behind a single word: *yes*.

The Battle

He closed his eyes. And the whispers began.

"It isn't really cheating. Everyone bends the rules. You've been fighting uphill your whole life — why shouldn't you level the field?"

The voice was silky, almost reasonable. He could already imagine rationalizations: the system was unjust, the professor unfair, life itself tilted against him. Who would know? Who would lose?

But another voice — quieter, yet heavier — rose from deeper within. *"Truth is not optional. It is your spine. If you sell it, you will walk bent forever."*

He remembered a line from the Gemara he had studied years before: *"Truth is the seal of the Ribbono Shel Olam."* To surrender to falsehood now would be to erase that seal from his own life, to exchange eternal currency for counterfeit paper.

And yet — the fears gnawed. He saw his wife, clutching their newborn, and the rent notice sliding under the door. He heard his father's voice: *"If you lose the scholarship, how will you manage?"*

The phone buzzed again, insistent, almost mocking.

"Well? Do you want it or not?"

The Turning Point

David stared at the device. His thumb hovered. He could end the torment with a single tap.

But then he saw something else in his mind: his children, asleep in their beds years from now. He imagined leaning over them, whispering goodnight, knowing that the bread on the table came from deceit. Could he look them in the eye and call himself their father, their teacher, if the very foundation beneath them was fraud?

His hand trembled, but his resolve hardened. He typed, letter by letter, as though chiseling stone:

"No thanks. I'll take the exam straight."

He pressed send before courage could leak away.

The reply came instantly: *"Suit yourself. Don't say I didn't offer."*

David set the phone down. His body sagged with exhaustion, but there was lightness too — the strange relief of a man who has thrown away counterfeit gold and reclaimed his own breath. He bent back over his notes, whispering a prayer that was half plea, half vow:

"Hashem, let me succeed with honesty — or not at all."

The Exam

Morning. The exam hall was a cavern of fluorescent light. Students filed in with faces drained of color, each carrying their secret fears like contraband. The professor distributed the thick packets with the gravity of a judge passing sentence.

David opened his copy. His heart lurched. The questions coiled with traps, twisting into unfamiliar territory. Around him, pens scratched frantically. Some students glanced down at their pages with eerie calm — too calm.

David fought to steady his breath. He wrote. He crossed out. He began again. Minutes became hours, the clock a whip at his back. By the end, his paper was blotched with sweat and ink, his mind a battlefield littered with doubts. He handed it in, not with triumph, but with the hollow resignation of a soldier leaving the field uncertain if he had won or lost.

The Aftermath

Two weeks later, grades appeared. He stared at the screen, scarcely breathing. **B+.** Not dazzling, not heroic. But enough. The scholarship remained.

Yet the true reward came months later. After a lecture, the professor — a severe man, known for his suspicion — called him aside. His eyes, sharp as chisels, studied David.

"Stein," he said, voice low. "I know who cheated. Many did. You didn't. That matters more to me than numbers. Have you thought about graduate school? I'd recommend you."

David walked out of the building dazed, almost trembling. He had nearly sold his soul for a handful of exam points. And instead, integrity had opened a door that dishonesty never could.

Reflection

Falsehood promises ease but leaves you hollow. Truth feels costly, yet it builds foundations that endure storms.

As Chazal teach: *"The world stands on three things: on judgment, on truth, and on peace."* (Avot 1:18)

That exam did not merely preserve his scholarship; it engraved his life. For in that moment of trembling defiance, when he whispered "no" to the easy lie, David sealed himself to the oldest covenant of all: to live — and perhaps to suffer — beneath the uncompromising light of truth.

The Song in the Hospital Room

"Serve Hashem with joy."
(Tehillim 100:2)

The Setup

Winter had descended on Brooklyn with an unforgiving grip. The wind howled down the avenues, rattling windows and driving a damp chill into every corner. Inside a hospital ward that smelled faintly of antiseptic and muted despair, Reb Shlomo lay in a bed by the window. Pneumonia had weakened his lungs, and the IV in his arm seemed to drain his spirit as much as it infused his veins.

For decades, he had been known as the *ba'al niggun* of the neighborhood — the man who could lift a tired wedding crowd with a soaring melody, the one who infused every Shabbos table with warmth through zemiros. His voice was not merely sound; it was memory, devotion, prayer, and laughter woven into one. Now, lying beneath fluorescent lights, he felt stripped of that gift.

His children came in shifts, each trying to mask the dread in their eyes. They adjusted blankets, offered words of encouragement, and smiled as though smiles could drive away illness. One evening, when the room was quiet and shadows stretched long against the wall, he whispered to his daughter:

"I have no strength left. Even to daven feels like climbing a mountain whose peak I cannot see."

She clasped his hand, forcing a smile though tears gathered at the edges of her eyes. To her, this admission felt heavier than the machines beeping around him. The man of song, silenced.

The Battle

When the corridor lights dimmed and footsteps faded, the silence pressed hard. Shlomo stared at the plastic tubing that bound him to machinery. His thoughts grew dark. Perhaps my time is finished, he reasoned. What use is a voice that cannot sing?

Despair — sly, persuasive — whispered to him: *Why resist? Rest now. The world will manage without your melody.*

But deep within memory, another voice stirred. He heard again the words of his rebbi from long ago:

"Simchah is not a luxury; it is avodah. Joy is not the byproduct of an easy life. It is the very force that makes life bearable, that transforms pain into strength."

The words hovered like faint music, urging him to fight not with medicine or muscle, but with song.

The Turning Point

He closed his eyes and searched inwardly. At first, only a faint hum emerged, fragile and broken, almost like a child's whimper. But as his lips trembled, the hum gained shape, turning into a melody remembered from his youth:

"Kol ha'olam kulo, gesher tzar me'od — the whole world is but a narrow bridge, and the main thing is not to fear at all."

The notes cracked, the rhythm faltered, but the sound was unmistakable.

A nurse passing the doorway paused. His daughter, returning quietly with a cup of tea, froze in place. Her eyes widened — she had not expected to hear her father's voice rise in song again.

He beckoned weakly with a hand. "Sing with me," he whispered.

Her voice was shaky at first, tentative. Then it strengthened, rising to support his. The nurse, though unfamiliar with the words, joined in the tune. Slowly, the small, sterile room filled with harmony — fragile, imperfect, but radiant with defiance against despair.

The Aftermath

By Shabbos, the story had spread. Friends, neighbors, and even patients from other wards drifted into his room. They gathered around his bed, singing zemiros. The whitewashed walls seemed to echo with light. Doctors shook their heads, baffled by what they called "improved morale," though those present knew it was more than morale — it was spirit reclaiming dominion over body.

A week later, his breathing steadied. The infection loosened its grip. Discharge papers were signed, and Reb Shlomo returned home, thinner, weaker — yet luminous. That first Shabbos back, his neighbors filled the dining room. When he led *Birkat Hamazon*, tears coursed down his face.

"Despair nearly captured me," he confessed afterward. "But joy — even broken, whispered joy — chased it away. Hashem does not need flawless voices; He seeks hearts that still wish to sing."

Reflection

Sadness is a thief, draining life of its color. Joy is not naïve denial of suffering, but holy resistance to it — the declaration that even amidst weakness, Hashem remains our melody.

As the Rambam writes (*Hilchot Lulav 8:15*):

"The joy one feels in serving Hashem is a great and lofty form of avodah."

And so, in a hospital room that once smelled only of antiseptic and loss, a broken melody rose. It was not polished, not strong, but it carried eternity — proof that even at the edge of silence, song can still be born.

The Broken Pitcher: Gratitude in Loss (הכרת הטוב)

"טוֹב לְהוֹדוֹת לַה'."
"It is good to give thanks to Hashem." (Tehillim 92:2)

The Dawn of the Market

The alley behind the shuk stirred awake before the sun lifted its face. First came the smells: yeast-breath rising from the baker's stone oven, figs bruising sweetly in their baskets, the tang of wet rope and damp clay. Then came the sounds: wagon wheels creaking, a mule sighing with patient resignation, a woman humming as she folded linen across a wooden stall. And in that gray hour, when the world is stripped of ornament and still honest, a narrow-shouldered man named Yitzchak bent beneath a yoke and lifted two clay pitchers onto his back.

He walked with the careful steps of one who knows that what rests across his spine is not merely water but also livelihood, also dignity. The wooden yoke groaned like a tired companion. To the left hung a stout earthen pitcher cushioned with straw; to the right, its twin — except for the crack that curved faintly from lip to belly like a pale scar smiling at misfortune.

Yitzchak had discovered the fissure a month earlier. At first, he pretended it wasn't there. He twisted the jug this way and that, searching for an angle where the line looked like marble instead of ruin.

But by the time he returned from the spring each morning, a dark streak had crept down its side, and drops had dripped — bead by bead — leaving a ribbon of damp along the road, as though some invisible creature had passed before him, padding quietly through the dust.

"Yitzchak," the baker called one dawn, sliding loaves into the fiery mouth of the oven, "your pitcher is crying again."

Yitzchak smiled and hitched the yoke higher.
 "It is sentimental," he said. "It weeps for bread it cannot eat."

They laughed together, but laughter is a frail shield against the weight of worry. Each morning half the water he drew bled away before reaching the communal cistern. Half his wages. And the rent for the single room he shared with his mother gnawed at him sharper each week, like a smile that has stiffened and turned brittle.

The Weight of Debt

The spring lay beyond the city walls, a silver coin resting in the palm of rock. The path wound between low stone fences that coaxed reluctant soil to hold thorny bushes. Each dawn the same procession climbed: the vine-pruner with rope-burned palms; the herb-seller widow who greeted even stones; children with bare feet and loose tongues; and Yitzchak with his pair of pitchers, his ears filling with whispered prayers as he walked.

He recited *Modeh Ani* with his first steps, and saved *Ashrei* for the hill — using each word as a staff to steady him. But the day the landlord's nephew came to collect rent, that hill rose higher than Sinai.

"Your rent is late again," said the nephew, leaning on the doorframe, scraping dust from his beard with the edge of a coin. It was not cruelty, merely business — which often cuts colder than cruelty.

"I will pay," said Yitzchak. "Two days."

"That is what you said last week."

Yitzchak glanced inside, to where his mother slept, kerchief slipping over one eye. He thought of the crack that stole half his week's earnings. "Two days," he repeated. The nephew shrugged and left, taking with him what little warmth lingered in the room.

The Flowered Path

The next morning, the road to the spring was crowded. A pile of pomegranates had toppled, their split skins bleeding red across the stones. Yitzchak filled both pitchers, tied their corks tight, and started back up the hill. The heat pressed down like an interrogator's hand. The left pitcher sweated wholesomely; the right did as it had learned to do: it wept in steady drops.

By the time he reached the cistern, the cracked pitcher was light as shame. He delivered what he had, collected coins counted without a glance, and turned to leave. Then an old man stepped across his path, his face a map of deep lines, his robe that of a melamed, his smile that of a grandfather who has forgiven every foolish boy.

"Your pitcher leaks," he said, as though announcing a birth.

"I know," Yitzchak replied. "I am saving for a new one."

"Come," the old man said, nodding toward the road. "Walk with me."

They walked in silence, the yoke creaking between them like a lullaby. At the bend where the path met the garden plots, the melamed stopped and pointed to the right-hand verge.

"Look."

Yitzchak saw it then: the right side of the road — the side beneath the leaking pitcher — was lined with blossoms. Tiny violets bowed shyly, yellow flowers laughed in the sun, grass grew thick as a child's curls after winter. The left side, beneath the whole pitcher, was nothing but dust and thorn.

"I don't understand," Yitzchak said.

"Your pitcher bleeds," the old man explained gently, "and the earth drinks. Don't be swifter than Hashem in calling something waste. Sometimes what seeps from us without our consent is watering fields we cannot yet see."

Yitzchak's throat, which all week had been a fence, felt suddenly like a gate.

The Trial of the Storm

The days that followed strung themselves like beads: fill, climb, deliver, listen. Gratitude crept into his steps: for the way one drop darkened dust to near black; for the way a rope slackened when he sang to it; for the way his mother's lips curved in sleep. Gratitude did not pay the rent, but it warmed the hands that counted coins.

On the last day of the month, a storm prowled the horizon. The market tied down its awnings with curses and laughter. Delayed by helping an old woman draw from the public well, Yitzchak reached the spring under a sky grown heavy. He filled his pitchers and started the ascent as the first drops — fat as promises — struck the ground.

At the narrowest curve, the vine-pruner's mule spooked at thunder. Wheels skidded, the cart tilted toward the precipice. The man's cry was the thin crack of a breaking branch. Instinct moved quicker than thought: Yitzchak dropped the yoke, lunged, and braced his shoulder against the cart. His muscles were rope, his breath torn parchment, but his weight — paltry as he thought of it — was enough to halt the slide until others rushed to help. Together they steadied the load; the mule quieted; the danger passed. The pruner collapsed in the mud and laughed as though he had found a ring lost in childhood.

"You saved my grapes and my bones," he said, clapping Yitzchak's shoulder with a palm that smelled of sap. "Name your price."

Panting, Yitzchak looked back down the path. His sturdy pitcher lay shattered, its shards like a star chart of some unknown country. The cracked one — the flawed, patient one — rested whole among flowers, beaded with defiant drops.

"I have no price," Yitzchak said softly. "But if you wish, buy from the widows this week. Pay them more than they ask."

The Reward Unforeseen

He delivered half a pitcher beneath a sky stitched with lightning. The quartermaster, usually brisk and cold, lingered.

"I saw what happened," he said, counting coins. "And I've watched that right-side verge for weeks. Yesterday the city council voted to plant fig saplings there. 'The soil is better on the right,' I told them, though I did not know why. Now I do. They want someone to water the trees through summer. Slow work, steady pay. A man who knows how to spill just enough."

He pushed the coins across the plank, then added two more.
"For your rent," he said.

"Why?" Yitzchak asked, hesitant, as a man starved hesitates before a feast.

The quartermaster shrugged. "Because your pitcher leaks. And because when you braced that cart, my son was beneath it."

Yitzchak closed his eyes. *"Baruch HaTov VeHaMetiv,"* he whispered. Blessed is the Good Who does good.

Epilogue

Weeks later, fig saplings lined the path where flowers had grown. Yitzchak took the job of watering them. His cracked pitcher — faithful now as an old dog — leaked along the way, and he no longer tried to stop it. In time, the trees bore fruit. Children plucked sweetness on their way to cheder; brides and grooms found shade on the road to the chuppah. What had been a strip of dust became a living sentence that the city read in summer and remembered in winter.

Years later, when the melamed passed away, Yitzchak brought a ripe fig to the house of mourning. He told the story of the crack and the flowers, and the mourners laughed the good laugh that cleans a room without opening a window.

On his way home he paused at the first fig tree, laid his palm against its bark, and whispered the verse the old man had loved to teach to wide-eyed boys:

"Give thanks to Hashem, for He is good; His kindness endures forever." (Tehillim 136:1)

And above him, the leaves clapped their hands in agreement.

Musar Takeaway — Hakarat HaTov

You never know where your lack, your "leak," is watering fields unseen. Often the crack in your pitcher — the loss, the delay, the pain — is the very channel through which Hashem nourishes life, for others and, in time, for you as well. Our task is to give thanks, to keep walking, and to remain open to the goodness that flows from the break.

The Rabbi and the Thief: Patience that Transforms (סבלנות)

"הֱוֵי מְתוּנִים בַּדִּין."
"Be patient in judgment." (Pirkei Avot 1:1)

The Night of the Break-In

The marketplace had been asleep for hours. The cries of merchants and the rustle of coin had given way to the hush of moonlight; wooden shutters, once rattling in the day's bargaining wind, now clung tight to silence. In a crooked little house at the edge of the square lived Rabbi Eliezer, known throughout the town as a man who carried Torah in one hand and kindness in the other. To his students, he was the one who could strike fire from damp wood, who could coax sparks of holiness from souls others dismissed as ash.

But that night, his own flame was put to the test.

A window creaked. The rabbi stirred, listening. A shadow slid across the floor, awkward, unsteady, as though the darkness itself had lent clumsy legs to desperation. His eyes adjusted: a man, clothes threadbare, cuff torn, hands rifling through drawers that contained little more than crumbs of parchment and prayer.

The rabbi could have cried out. He could have summoned neighbors, who would have stormed in with fists and curses, or seized a stick to defend his home. Instead, he cleared his throat softly, a sound gentler than a rebuke.

"Son," he said into the stillness, "you look hungry. Before you take anything, sit. Eat."

The intruder froze, as though struck. His heart pounded against his ribs. "Eat?" he whispered. "I came to steal, not to beg."

But the rabbi had already risen. His candle painted calm, golden circles on the rough walls. From a cupboard he drew bread, olives, and a small jug of water. He laid them upon the table as though welcoming a guest rather than confronting a thief.

"No man can think straight with an empty stomach," he said simply. "Eat first. Then we will talk."

The Bread of Hesitation

The thief stood suspended between shame and appetite. His fingers twitched, hovering over the bread as though it might bite him back. Finally, with the trembling of one who has long been starved of kindness, he lowered himself onto the bench and tore off a crust. The crackle of bread in the quiet room sounded louder than thunder.

They sat together in silence, one eating, one watching. Only when the man wiped his mouth on his sleeve did Rabbi Eliezer speak again.

"My son," he began, "your hands are strong. Strong enough to build, not merely to take. Tomorrow, come to me in daylight. I will find you honest work."

The thief barked a bitter laugh. "Work? Who would trust me? Tonight you saw what I am."

The rabbi met his eyes — not with the hard glare of a judge, but with the softness of one who remembers childhood wounds. "No," he said. "Tonight I saw what hunger can make of a man. That is not who you are."

The thief's gaze dropped. No one had ever spoken to him as though he were more than his worst deed.

The Turning Point

He rose, expecting a threat, a demand, perhaps the warning of authorities. Instead, the rabbi only nodded toward the loaf.

"Take the bread with you," he said. "And remember — you will always find a place at my table."

The thief stumbled into the night, clutching bread he had not stolen. That weight pressed heavier than silver.

The next day, he did not return. Nor the next. Shame is a prison with bars stronger than iron. But on the third morning, as Rabbi Eliezer mended a broken fence in his yard, a shadow fell across the ground.

"I am here," the man muttered, eyes fixed on the dust.

The rabbi handed him a hammer. "Then let us begin."

A New Life

The work was slow, clumsy at first: hauling water, chopping wood, fixing fences. The man's back ached, but his heart — once hardened — began to soften under the steady rhythm of being treated not as a criminal, but as a human being. Rabbi Eliezer paid him fairly, spoke to him with dignity, and never once mentioned the night of the break-in.

Weeks later, as they sat by the fire after a long day's labor, the rabbi placed a hand upon his shoulder.

"You thought you came here to steal silver," he said gently. "But perhaps Hashem sent you to steal something far greater — to steal your own life back from the grip of the yetzer hara. And for that, I thank you."

Tears welled in the man's eyes. He whispered, "Rebbe, you have stolen me back... from myself."

In time, the man became one of the rabbi's most devoted students. In the beit midrash, no one remembered him as the thief who crept in the night. He was known instead as a *baal teshuvah*, a man whose patience with others was as expansive as the patience once shown to him.

Reflection

The rabbi's patience did not merely prevent another crime; it unlocked the door to redemption. Where most would have seen only the act, he chose to see the man.

True *savlanut* is not weakness, but strength — the deliberate choice to restrain anger when anger feels justified. In that restraint lies the power to transform a thief into a student, a night of sin into a lifetime of Torah.

The Candle of Forgiveness: Lighting the Darkness (Mechilah)

"The soul of man is the candle of Hashem."
(Mishlei 20:27)

The Grudge That Would Not Die

Yom Kippur had descended upon the shtetl like a blanket of holiness. The synagogue shimmered with the gentle glow of hundreds of candles, their still flames standing guard over the prayers of trembling souls. The air was thick with melody and tears — whispers of confession rising and falling like waves of longing. Even the cobblestone streets outside seemed hushed, as though the entire world awaited judgment.

But not every heart inside was calm.

In a corner stood Reb Mendel, the wealthiest merchant in town. His white kittel gleamed, but his heart was darkened with hurt. For months, he had carried resentment toward his neighbor, a humble tailor who had once mocked him in public. The words were small, yet the wound festered. While others swayed in prayer, Mendel's heart refused to move. His lips spoke the *Vidui*, but the words hung lifeless, like smoke that could not rise.

The Rabbi's Message

After *Kol Nidrei*, when most had left and the synagogue was wrapped in stillness, the rabbi approached Mendel. He did not carry a candle — for it is forbidden to move one on Yom Kippur — but he stopped beside a flickering light already standing on the table.

"Mendel," he began softly, his voice like a father's, "why does your face remain so troubled on the Day when Hashem opens the gates of mercy?"

Mendel sighed. "How can I forgive him, Rabbi? He shamed me before others. If I pardon him, I lose my honor. If I hold my grudge, at least I keep my dignity."

The rabbi looked toward the flame on the table. "Do you see that candle?" he asked.
Mendel nodded.

"Imagine," said the rabbi, "if you were to cover it tightly, hiding its light because of anger or pride. What would happen?"

Mendel hesitated. "It would go out — or burn what covers it."

The rabbi smiled sadly. "Exactly so. When you hide the light of forgiveness, it burns only you. Anger and grudges are like fire trapped in the heart. But when you allow the light to shine freely — when you forgive — you do not lose honor. You regain your peace."

The Inner Struggle

Mendel looked at the unmoving flame. Though the rabbi had not touched it, its steady glow seemed to pierce through him. In that light he saw the truth — his pain, his pride, his smallness before Heaven.

He remembered days when others had forgiven *him* for harsh words spoken in haste. He remembered his father's saying:
"Better to lose a coin than to lose a friend; better to lose a friend than to lose your soul."

Tears began to fall. "If I forgive him," he whispered, "will Hashem forgive me?"

The rabbi placed a hand on his shoulder. "Hashem mirrors the heart, Mendel. If you open yours to mercy, Heaven will open its gates to you."

The Light Restored

When dawn broke and the *Ne'ilah* prayers approached, the congregation gathered once more. Mendel rose, trembling, and walked across the shul to where the tailor stood wrapped in his tallit. The crowd fell silent.

"My brother," Mendel said, his voice breaking, "I forgive you. May Heaven forgive us both."

The tailor's eyes filled with tears. They embraced — two souls who had released their burdens. Their prayers rose together, pure and strong.

Some swore that the candles in the synagogue glowed more brightly at that moment, though no one had touched them. Perhaps it was not the wax that burned brighter, but the hearts of men made whole again.

Musar Reflection

One who refuses to forgive carries a hidden fire that burns his own soul. Forgiveness, by contrast, releases the flame to shine freely — bringing warmth both to the forgiver and the forgiven.

Takeaway: True dignity is not found in holding on to hurt but in releasing it. When you let go of anger, you make room for Hashem's light to dwell within you.

The Silent Victory: Mastery of the Self (כיבוש היצר)

"Who is mighty? One who conquers his inclination." (Pirkei Avot 4:1)

Market Day in Krakow

The market square of Krakow was alive with clamor and color. Merchants shouted prices across the throng, their voices rasping like trumpets above the din. Women balanced baskets of cabbages and carrots on their heads, weaving through the crowd with practiced grace. Chickens protested from wicker cages, their feathers flying as if to punctuate the tumult. The mingled scents of roasted chestnuts, damp straw, and sweat hung thick in the winter air.

Among the chaos walked Rabbi Shimon, a figure of calm amid the storm. His presence was well-known in the city: a scholar with a mind as sharp as glass and a tongue as gentle as silk. He had come not for trade but to meet a student after prayer. Yet fate—or perhaps Providence—had other designs for him that day.

From the far end of the square staggered a man, drunk to the bone. His coat hung lopsided, his hair a nest of disorder, his eyes glassy pools of inebriation. His voice, cracked and raw, suddenly pierced the air.

"There he is!" he slurred, thrusting a wavering finger at the rabbi. "The holy scholar! The saintly fraud!"

The square turned to look. The market thrives on spectacle, and scandal is sweeter than spice.

The Insults

The drunk lurched forward, his breath sour with spirits. "Look at him," he jeered, swaying on unsteady legs. "Draped in his pious robes, thinking himself higher than the rest of us! I know his type—better than thou, holier-than-thou!"

Then, with theatrical contempt, he spat on the ground near Rabbi Shimon's feet.

Gasps rippled through the crowd. A murmur of outrage rose—*"Shame! To insult a rabbi in public!"* Yet others, hungry for drama, leaned forward, eager to see the holy man's response.

Rabbi Shimon's face burned crimson. His fists tightened within the folds of his sleeves. Inside his chest, anger struck its war drum: *How dare he? Before the people? Shall I let my honor be trampled like mud beneath his boots?*

Hundreds of eyes bored into him, awaiting the clash.

The Pause

Time slowed. A silence stretched taut as a drawn bowstring. Rabbi Shimon drew in a breath, then another. In that fragile pause, he heard, as if from long ago, his father's voice: *"Strength is not in the hand that strikes, but in the heart that restrains."*

His fists loosened. His jaw unclenched. His lips pressed together—not in fury, but in discipline.

And then—he said nothing.

The Crowd's Restlessness

The drunk, sensing the void, shouted louder, flailing his arms like a drowning man. But his insults fell into Rabbi Shimon's silence like stones into deep water—vanishing without echo.

The crowd shifted uneasily. One merchant whispered, "The rabbi's silence is answer enough." Another murmured, "He has defeated him without uttering a word."

Starved of reaction, the drunk faltered. His voice cracked, his certainty wavered. With a shrug, he turned, stumbling back into the alleys that had birthed him.

The Aftermath

A young student approached, eyes wide with awe. "Rebbe," he asked, "why did you not answer him? A man must defend his honor!"

Rabbi Shimon turned his calm gaze toward the boy. "When a dog barks at the king," he asked softly, "does the king bark back? My silence was not weakness—it was a battle. Not against him, but against my own yetzer that begged me to shout. And by Hashem's mercy, I won."

The student bowed his head, realizing that in the crowded marketplace he had just witnessed a lesson greater than any sermon delivered in the beit midrash.

The Hidden Fruit

Weeks later, there came a knock at the rabbi's door. It was the drunkard—sober now, his eyes clouded with shame. He bowed deeply, voice trembling.

"Rebbe," he whispered, "your silence burned me more than a hundred curses. That night I saw myself for what I was—and I could not bear it. Forgive me."

Rabbi Shimon lifted him gently. "My brother, I had nothing to forgive. My struggle was never with you, but with myself. And with Heaven's help, I prevailed."

The man wept openly. From that day forward he became a regular in the synagogue. The noisy eruptions of his drunkenness were replaced by whispered prayers, as though silence itself had become his teacher.

Musar Reflection

Hebrew:

הגיבור האמיתי איננו זה שמנצח אחרים, אלא זה שמנצח את יצרו. שתיקתו של הרב לא הייתה חולשה אלא כוח—הכוח לא לתת לאחר להכתיב את דרכו.

Translation:

The true hero is not he who conquers others, but he who conquers himself. The rabbi's silence was not weakness but strength—the strength to refuse another the power to dictate his path.

Takeaway:

Honor defended in anger is fleeting. Honor preserved through restraint endures forever.

The Weight of a Single Word: The Power of Speech (Shmirat HaLashon)

"Death and life are in the power of the tongue."
(Mishlei 18:21)

The Whisper in the Market

In the bustling town of Lublin, the market was the living heart of the community. Vendors shouted the merits of their wares, children wove between baskets and barrels, and every narrow alley buzzed with rumor as much as with trade. It was here, in the swirl of noise and color, that a single careless word began a journey that would wound more deeply than any blade.

Chaim the innkeeper, wearied after a long morning, leaned across his counter to a passing traveler and muttered:
"Do you know Reb Zalman, the merchant? They say his scales are not altogether honest."

He meant little by it—perhaps only to fill the air with talk, perhaps to amuse himself. But words, once released, have no leash. This one slipped from his lips like a spark borne on the wind. By nightfall, it had leapt from ear to ear, from home to home. Soon the town murmured with a single refrain: *"Zalman cheats with his scales."*

The Ruin of a Reputation

Within days, Zalman felt the chill. Loyal customers turned aside. Friends who once greeted him now avoided his gaze. When he entered the beit midrash, the hum of learning faltered, and men shifted uneasily on their benches. Business dwindled, and shame clung to him like an unwashed garment.

At last, broken and bewildered, Zalman sought the rav of Lublin. His voice quivered as he spoke:
 "Rebbe, I have never defrauded a man of a single coin. Yet now the town looks upon me as a thief."

The rav, a man whose eyes were deep with both mercy and judgment, listened in silence. Then he sent for Chaim the innkeeper.

The Rav's Lesson

When Chaim arrived, still puzzled, the rav said:
 "Take a pillow filled with feathers. Bring it to the marketplace, tear it open, and then return to me."

Though confused, Chaim obeyed. In the square, he ripped the pillow, and the wind caught the feathers, scattering them like snow. They danced across rooftops, swirled into alleyways, drifted beyond the town into open fields.

Chaim returned, the remnants still clinging to his sleeves. "I have done as you asked, Rebbe."

"Good," said the rav. "Now go—and gather every feather back into the pillow."

Chaim's mouth fell open. "But that is impossible! The wind has carried them everywhere!"

The rav's voice was calm but cut sharper than steel:
 "So too with your word. You thought it small, harmless. Yet it scattered across the town. Can you recall it? Can you mend the harm to Reb Zalman's name?"

The Burden of Regret

Color drained from Chaim's face. He turned to Zalman, tears filling his eyes.
 "Forgive me! I spoke without thought, and now see the ruin it has caused!"

Zalman's lips trembled. "I forgive you," he whispered. "But my name—who will restore it whole?"

The rav placed a hand on both their shoulders.
 "This is why the Torah warns with such severity against lashon hara. Words are like arrows: once loosed, they cannot be recalled. Yet just as one word can wound, another—uttered with truth and humility—can begin to heal. From this day forward, Chaim, you must speak in Zalman's honor wherever you go. Let your tongue, which scattered feathers of darkness, now scatter feathers of light."

The Healing

So it was. Chaim, chastened and broken by remorse, became the loudest defender of Zalman's integrity. To every traveler and townsman he proclaimed:

"Do business with Reb Zalman! His scales are truer than the sun itself!"

Slowly, trust returned. Customers came back. And though his reputation bore a scar, Zalman's dignity was not destroyed.

As for Chaim, never again did he speak lightly. Until the end of his days, he told children and students the parable of the feathers, urging them to guard their tongues as one guards treasure.

Musar Reflection

A word spoken carelessly flies like a bird that cannot be recalled. But when the tongue is used for good, it can spread light as easily as it once spread darkness.

Takeaway: Guarding the tongue is not only about refraining from harm. It is about choosing speech that heals, honors, and uplifts.

The Lost Purse: Honesty Beyond the Test (יֹשֶׁר)

"דַּבֵּר אֱמֶת בִּלְבָבוֹ."
"He speaks truth in his heart." (Tehillim 15:2)

The Discovery

The streets of Warsaw glittered beneath a stubborn frost. Snow clung to the uneven cobblestones like a thin blanket refusing to be shaken off, and carriages rattled cautiously, their horses steaming in the frigid air. Yosef the cobbler drew his patched shawl tighter around his shoulders as he trudged homeward from the beit midrash, hands roughened by leather and by prayer alike.

At the mouth of a narrow alley, his boot struck against something soft. He stooped and found a leather purse heavy in his palm. A single glance inside made his breath seize: gold coins, more than he had ever seen in his life. Enough to feed his family for years. Enough to pull him forever out of the shadow of poverty.

His stomach growled at the thought of meat on Shabbos, his children shod in new boots, medicine for his ailing wife. But then came a whisper within: *This is not yours.*

The Temptation

That night Yosef sat at the small wooden table in his dimly lit home, the purse before him like an unwanted guest. Above him, in the loft, his children slept under threadbare blankets, their shallow breathing rising like fragile petitions. From the other room came the harsh cough of his wife.

The purse seemed almost to glow in the candlelight, each coin a promise of relief.
 The yetzer within him argued: *Who would know? Perhaps Heaven itself has sent this gift. You too deserve respite.*

But his heart recalled the verse: *"Keep far from falsehood."* He had not earned this money. To keep it would be theft cloaked in rationalization.

By dawn his decision was carved in stone.

The Test

Yosef carried the purse to the magistrate's office, where all lost goods were announced. Before long a wealthy merchant rushed in, his face pale and damp with worry.

"My purse!" the man cried, clutching it with trembling hands. "I thought it lost beyond recovery!"

Turning to Yosef he asked, "Did you open it?"

"I did," Yosef admitted. "I saw what was inside."

"And yet you returned it?" The merchant's voice cracked with disbelief. "Do you know what this means? Those coins were the wages of dozens of workers. Without them, their families would have starved. You returned not merely gold—you returned life."

The Ripple

Word spread swiftly through Warsaw: the poor cobbler who had found a fortune and returned it untouched.

Soon customers thronged his small workshop, eager to entrust their shoes to hands that stitched not only leather but truth.

A student once asked him:

"Reb Yosef, was it not difficult? Did you not think of your hunger?"

Yosef smiled wearily. "Every night I hear my children ask for bread. But I could never endure hearing them, years from now, called the children of a thief. Poverty passes. A stained name does not."

The Reward Beyond Coin

Weeks later the merchant returned, this time bearing not gold but opportunity: a steady contract to repair the boots of his laborers. Yosef's little shop flourished. He never became rich, but never again did his children go to bed hungry.

And in the beit midrash, when Yosef entered with calloused hands and a quiet smile, the students whispered one to another:
"There goes a man who speaks truth in his heart."

Musar Reflection

In Hebrew:
האדם נבחן לא רק ברגעי עוני, אלא גם בשעה שניתנת בידו האפשרות ליטול שלא כדין. היושר הנשמר בלב קשה – בונה עולם שלם.

Translation:
A person is tested not only in times of scarcity, but in the moments when dishonesty seems easy and even justified. Honesty, guarded stubbornly in the heart, builds a world of trust.

Takeaway:
True wealth is not counted in coins that jingle in the pocket, but in the integrity that rests unshaken in the heart.

The Coat on the Road: Chesed Without Measure (חֶסֶד)

"Olam chesed yibaneh."
"The world is built on kindness." (Tehillim 89:3)

The Frozen Road

The winter of 1872 pressed down upon Galicia with a merciless hand. Snow descended day after day, smothering sound, swallowing color, turning the world into a white silence. Travelers trudged like phantoms through the drifts, their breaths pluming in the air.

On the road between two villages walked Reb Dovid, a timber merchant by trade. His fur-lined coat shielded him from the piercing wind, and his boots crunched steadily in the snow. He was not a man of wealth, yet his business gave him modest comfort: a hearth that glowed, bread upon the table, warmth for his family.

Rounding a bend near the forest, he noticed a shape half-buried in snow. At first glance it seemed nothing more than a fallen log from a passing cart. But then it stirred. A groan escaped. It was no log, but a man—thin as twigs, clothing in tatters, face blue with the creeping frost.

Reb Dovid bent low.
 "Brother! What are you doing here? You will freeze!"

The man's lips moved faintly.

"On my way… to Tarnow… collapsed…"

The Test of Chesed

Reb Dovid looked up and down the road. No traveler in sight. No inn within reach. To lift the man alone would be near impossible, and the storm pressed heavier with every breath.

He thought of home—his wife waiting with the evening meal, his children eager for their father's tales. And then he thought of the coat on his back—the barrier between himself and death's cold breath.

His heart wavered: *If I surrender my coat, will I not condemn myself? Yet if I hold it, surely he will perish.*

The verse echoed in his mind: *"Olam chesed yibaneh."* The world endures only upon kindness. How, then, could he let it crumble here, on this desolate road?

Without another thought, he pulled off his coat, wrapped it tightly around the stranger's shivering frame, bent down, and heaved the man upon his shoulders. Then he began the long walk toward the village.

The Long Walk

Each step was torment. The wind knifed through his shirt; his body quaked in the storm. The man upon his back was dead weight, groaning faintly, near lifeless. Reb Dovid's breath came in ragged clouds, his legs burning with the effort. Yet within, a strange fire sustained him—whether faith, whether purpose, or perhaps the unseen arms of Hashem bearing him up.

At last, after what seemed like unending hours, lantern lights flickered in the distance. The village inn. He stumbled through the door, collapsing to the floor with the stranger still swaddled in his coat.

The innkeeper and his wife rushed forward, laid the frozen man near the fire, rubbed warmth into his limbs, and pressed hot tea against his lips. Slowly, color returned, and life glimmered again where death had encamped.

The Revelation

Only after the stranger slept did Reb Dovid think to ask his name. The innkeeper, curious, searched the man's satchel. Inside were papers marked with a crest: he was no beggar, but a wealthy merchant from Tarnow who had been stripped and robbed by bandits on the road.

When morning came, the merchant awoke. His eyes filled with tears as they fell upon Reb Dovid.
 "You saved me," he whispered. "Your coat was my life."

Reb Dovid smiled faintly.
 "It was only a coat."

But the merchant shook his head.

"No—it was more. It was your warmth, your strength, your kindness. I owe you everything."

The Reward Beyond Intention

Months later, Reb Dovid received a letter. Enclosed was a deed to a timber contract with generous terms, signed by the very man he had saved. *"This is but a fraction,"* the letter read, *"of the coat that gave me back my life."*

Yet Reb Dovid never recounted this part of the tale. When neighbors asked him about his newfound prosperity, he would answer only: "The world is built on kindness. What I gave returned to me in ways I never sought."

Musar Reflection

True kindness does not weigh its cost; it weighs the life of another. The world endures by such moments—when a man gives up his own warmth so that another may live.

Takeaway: Chesed that demands nothing is simple. Chesed that requires sacrifice—that risks something real—is holy.

The Broken Chair: Humility in Honor (Anavah)

"The reward of humility is fear of Hashem."
(Mishlei 22:4)

The Celebration

In the town of Pinsk, the synagogue gleamed as though dressed for a wedding. After years of sacrifice and communal effort, the new *aron kodesh* was finally complete—oak carved with exquisite care, silver letters inlaid like starlight. The people gathered for its dedication: candles flickered in glass holders, melodies soared to the rafters, and even the poorest among them wore their finest coats for the occasion.

At the center sat their leader, Rabbi Moshe. His reputation stretched far beyond the shtetl—renowned as a master of halakhah, a *posek* whose rulings guided merchants and shoemakers alike. Yet those who knew him best loved him not for his erudition but for the gentleness in his eyes when a child tugged at his sleeve.

On this night, the gabbai had prepared a special chair for him: new, sturdy, raised slightly higher than the others. "The Rav should be honored," he explained. "Let all see whom Heaven has blessed with Torah."

The Crack

When Rabbi Moshe lowered himself into the seat, a faint crack splintered the air. He remained still, smile frozen, while the wood beneath him trembled. Someone in the crowd chuckled nervously; another stifled a laugh.

And then, with a groan, the chair gave way.

The rabbi tumbled to the floor, his robes in disarray, his hat rolling across the stone tiles. Gasps erupted. Some covered their mouths; others stared in stunned silence, uncertain whether to rush forward or retreat from the awkwardness.

It was a moment saturated with humiliation. Another man might have flushed with fury, stormed out, or demanded silence.

But Rabbi Moshe rose slowly, brushed the dust from his cloak, retrieved his hat... and looked at the wreckage of the chair. Then, to everyone's astonishment, he laughed—a deep, genuine laugh that filled the hall like sunlight breaking through clouds.

The Lesson in the Laughter

"My friends," he said, lifting a broken leg of the chair, "see how Heaven reminds us? Even a rabbi sits only upon wood. And wood, like man, sometimes breaks."

The laughter spread—first tentative, then free—until the entire synagogue shook with joy. What might have been shame became relief, what might have fractured dignity became unity and warmth.

Rabbi Moshe went on: "Better that my chair should break than my heart. Better that pride should fall than peace between us. Let us dedicate not only this *aron kodesh*, but ourselves—to humility before Hashem."

After the Fall

From that night on, the tale of the broken chair passed from lip to lip in Pinsk. Children whispered it as a joke in the marketplace, merchants repeated it in jest between bargains, but always with admiration. "Did you hear? Our rabbi fell—and turned it into Torah!"

Visitors came expecting severity, but instead found a man whose humility made them stand taller. His greatness was not diminished by the fall; it was crowned by it.

And Rabbi Moshe himself? He had the chair repaired and placed in his private study, where it stood as a daily reminder: honor is fragile, but humility endures.

Musar Reflection

Hebrew:
הכבוד נופל ברגע, אך הענווה מחזיקה לעד. מי שיודע לצחוק על עצמו הופך בושה ללימוד, וחולשה לכוח.

Translation:
Honor may collapse in an instant, but humility endures forever. One who can laugh at himself transforms shame into teaching and weakness into strength.

Takeaway:
The truly honored are not those who sit upon tall chairs, but those who can rise with grace when the chair breaks beneath them.

The Widow's Loaf: Gratitude in Poverty

"It is good to give thanks to Hashem."
(Tehillim 92:2)

The Hunger

In a small shtetl outside Vilna lived Rivka, a widow with three children. Her husband had died young, leaving behind little more than a tiny oven, a few hens, and debts that gnawed at her soul like hidden mice in the walls.

Each day she baked bread to sell at the market, using the last of her flour for tomorrow's dough. It was never enough. Too often her children went to bed hungry, their frail arms curled around their empty bellies like question marks in the dark.

One bitter winter evening, Rivka counted her coins and found she had only enough for a single sack of flour. As she mixed the dough with tears, she whispered:
 —"Master of the Universe, You are the Father of orphans and the Judge of widows. Do not forget us."

The Stranger

As the bread baked, a knock came at the door. On the threshold stood an old beggar, his beard crusted with frost, his hands trembling.

—"Good woman," he said hoarsely, "I have not eaten in two days. Could you spare me a loaf?"

Rivka's heart tightened. To give him bread meant her own children might starve. To turn him away meant betraying everything her late husband had taught her: *A Jewish home must always have room for another.*

She looked at her children's wide eyes, then at the man's hollow face. Slowly, she lifted the largest loaf from the oven and placed it in his hands.

Tears welled in his eyes. "May the G-d of Israel bless you," he whispered, disappearing into the snow.

The Empty Cupboard

That night her children whimpered in hunger, and Rivka wept silently.
—"Perhaps I was a fool," she thought. "I gave away the little we had."

Before dawn she rose to knead what she thought was the last of the flour. But when she opened the cupboard, she froze. Where the night before there had been only dust, now stood a fresh sack of flour—white, full, and waiting.

She touched it with trembling hands, then fell to her knees in gratitude.

The Return of the Stranger

Later that week she saw the beggar again, this time in the market—not in rags, but in a modest merchant's coat. He came to her stall and purchased every loaf.

—"Why?" Rivka asked in wonder.

He smiled.
 —"Because you gave when you had nothing. Many give from wealth; you gave from hunger. That is a gift Heaven multiplies."

From then on, he returned often—sometimes as a customer, sometimes slipping coins into the hands of her children. Some whispered he was Eliyahu HaNavi in disguise. Others said only: *He was the answer to her prayer.*

Musar Reflection

Gratitude does not depend on abundance but on the heart. One who gives and thanks even in want discovers that Hashem's kindness is without limit.

Takeaway: True gratitude is born not when the cupboard is full, but when we can still say *"thank You"* with an empty hand.

The Empty Seat: Compassion Over Anger *(Rachamim)*

"As a man chastises his son, so Hashem your G-d chastises you."
(Devarim 8:5)

The Study Hall

In the great yeshiva of Pressburg, the beit midrash breathed with life. Pages of Gemara turned like wings of birds in flight, voices rose and clashed, arguments sharpened and softened, and the very air seemed to vibrate with the passion of Torah.

Every bench was filled—except one. Toward the back, a chair stood empty, its table bare like a silent question in the midst of the storm of learning.

That was Yisrael's seat. He was a student of keen mind but restless spirit. Lately he had been seen lingering in taverns, wasting hours in idle laughter, drifting farther and farther from the path of the yeshiva. Whispers followed him like shadows: *"He is lost... the yetzer hara has conquered him..."*

Rabbi Avraham heard the whispers. And each day, his gaze wandered to the empty seat, and a quiet ache pressed deeper into his chest.

The Encounter

One evening, word reached him: Yisrael was again at the tavern. Some urged:

"Rebbe, go now! Rebuke him sharply, in public, so that others will fear and not follow his ways."

Rabbi Avraham rose from his desk, wrapped his cloak around his shoulders, and walked through the icy streets until he reached the tavern's door. From within came music, clinking mugs, and the coarse laughter of men without Torah.

There sat Yisrael in the corner, hunched over a half-empty cup, forcing a laugh that never reached his eyes.

When the rabbi entered, the room froze. All turned. Yisrael's face drained of color. He braced himself for humiliation, for condemnation, perhaps even expulsion.

Instead, Rabbi Avraham crossed the room quietly, drew out the chair opposite, and sat down.

The Words That Weren't Spoken

For a long moment he said nothing. The silence pressed harder than any rebuke. Finally, in a voice low and steady, he said:

"Yisrael, your seat in the beit midrash is waiting. Every day I see it. And every day it asks me: *'Where is my student?'*"

Yisrael's eyes burned. His voice cracked: "Rebbe, I cannot return. I have fallen too far."

The rabbi reached across the table and clasped his hand. "No one falls farther than Hashem's mercy can reach. Come home. Not for me, not for them—but for the Torah that still waits to hear your voice."

The Way Back

Tears welled. Before the astonished tavern, Yisrael bowed his head upon his rabbi's hand, like a child at his father's knee. Without another word, he rose and followed him into the cold night.

The next morning, the empty seat was filled once more. Whispers returned: *"How can he sit among us after what he has done?"* But Rabbi Avraham silenced them with a single look.

"He is not back because he is perfect," the rabbi said quietly. "He is back because he is trying. And that is greater than perfection."

In time, Yisrael became one of the strongest learners in the yeshiva, and later a teacher himself—always alert to the "empty seats" of others, always gentle in his rebuke.

Musar Reflection

In Hebrew:

לפעמים השתיקה והחיבוק משפיעים יותר מן התוכחה. לראות את הכסא הריק של יהודי ולקרוא לו לחזור באהבה — זהו רחמים אמיתיים.

Translation:

Sometimes silence and an outstretched hand do more than a hundred words of rebuke. To notice the empty seat of a fellow Jew and call him back with love—that is true compassion.

Takeaway: Harsh words may frighten, but compassion heals. The greatest rebuke is not condemnation but the quiet reminder:
"Your place is still waiting for you."

The Rain That Didn't Come: Faith in the Dry Season (Emunah)

"The righteous shall live by his faith."
(Chavakuk 2:4)

The Dry Fields

In the town of Mezeritch, the summer stretched on — cruel and unending. Clouds drifted by like indifferent strangers, offering not a single drop. The earth cracked, the stalks of wheat withered, and hope dried faster than the fields themselves. Farmers gathered in the marketplace, their faces lined with worry, their voices faint with despair.

Among them stood Reb Nachman, a poor farmer with only a small plot and a feeble ox. His neighbors shook their heads at his stubbornness.

"Sell your land, Nachman. Nothing will grow this year. Better to save the little you have than lose it all."

But Reb Nachman smiled, weary yet steadfast.

"The rain will come. Hashem has not forgotten us."

They scoffed. Faith is easy when the fields are green; it is far harder when all the eye can see is dust.

Seeds of Faith

One evening, while others hid their wheat seeds away for the following year, Nachman's children found him in the field, scattering kernels into the cracked earth.

"Papa!" they cried. "Why waste the seeds? There is no rain!"

With fingers rough as bark, he pressed the kernels into the soil.

"My children," he said, "if we wait for the rain before planting, the rain will find nothing here to awaken. Faith is planting when the sky is still empty. Hashem will provide."

His wife, standing in the doorway, felt fear twist inside her chest. But she saw the light in his eyes, and she held her tongue.

The Laughter of Neighbors

Days turned into weeks. Each time neighbors passed by his barren plot, they mocked.

"Look at the fool, watering dust with sweat. Does he think his prayers will change the heavens?"

But each morning, Nachman bent over the dry ground and whispered words of Tehillim. His neighbors shook their heads, yet sometimes — in the silence of night — they admitted to themselves that perhaps they envied him. For though his field was empty, his heart was not.

The First Drop

One dawn, as Nachman walked his furrows, a single drop struck his cheek. He looked up. The heavens, once hard as iron, had softened into a gray promise. Another drop, and another — until the skies split open.

The earth drank greedily. Nachman fell to his knees, tears mingling with rain.

"Master of the Universe," he whispered, "You never left me."

Within weeks, fresh green shoots pierced the soil. His field — once the object of scorn — became the only one in the village alive with wheat. And when harvest came, neighbors stood speechless as golden stalks swayed where they had seen only dust.

The Harvest of Faith

That year, many families in the town would have starved had Nachman not opened his barns. He gave freely, without hesitation.

"The same G-d who brought rain to my field," he said, "brings bread to all His children. Take, and bless His Name."

From that day, his neighbors no longer called him a fool. They called him a man of **emunah**.

Musar Reflection

Hebrew:

האמונה איננה להאמין כאשר הכול ברור, אלא לזרוע דווקא כשהשמיים ריקים. מי שבוטח בה׳ גם בשעת יובש — זוכה לראות ברכה למעלה מן הדעת.

Translation:

Emunah is not believing when everything is clear; it is sowing seeds when the sky is empty. One who trusts in Hashem even in the dry season merits blessings beyond imagination.

Takeaway: True emunah is not waiting for proof — it is acting with trust even before the proof arrives.

The Closed Shop: Faith and Shabbos

"Six days work shall be done, but the seventh is a Sabbath."
(Shemot 35:2)

The Merchant's Dilemma

In the bustling city of Odessa, commerce roared on Shabbos. Ships unloaded their cargo on Friday night, and by Saturday morning the markets were alive. Merchants flung open their shops, eager to sell fabrics, foods, and wares to the sailors before their wages disappeared into the taverns.

Yaakov, a simple cloth merchant, felt the sting of temptation deep in his heart. His shop was small, his children wore patched and mended clothing, and his wife stretched every kopeck to keep the home afloat. More than once, a neighbor whispered to him in passing:

— *"Yaakov, if only you opened on Shabbos, within a year you'd be a wealthy man."*

Each Shabbos he faced the same test: outside, the clamor of the street, the bargaining cries, the clink of coins changing hands. And inside — shutters closed, candles glowing, his children's gentle voices singing *Shalom Aleichem*.

Yet even amid the holiness, a difficult thought gnawed within: *Am I withholding bread from my children's mouths? Is my faith nothing but folly?*

The Test

One Shabbos afternoon, as the family sang their *zemirot*, a loud pounding rattled the door. A foreign trader stood there, a heavy purse at his side.

— *"I urgently need cloth!"* he cried. *"I'll pay you double your price."*

Yaakov shook his head.
 — *"Today is Shabbos. I cannot sell."*

— *"Then triple!"* the trader pressed.

Yaakov placed his hand firmly on his son's shoulder and said with steady voice:
 — *"Not for all the gold in Odessa."*

The trader cursed and stormed away. Yaakov's children stared at him wide-eyed. His wife's face paled, but in her eyes gleamed a quiet pride.

The Reward of Faith

The very next week, the same trader returned — this time on a weekday.

— *"I went to others,"* he admitted, *"but their cloth was poor. Yours has a reputation. I will buy your entire stock."*

The news spread quickly through Odessa: Yaakov was the merchant who would not sell on Shabbos. His cloth was excellent, yes — but more than that, his faith was worth more to him than fortune. Customers began to flock to his shop, some for his wares, others simply to trade with a man whose word was stronger than profit.

And so, his livelihood grew — not in spite of Shabbos, but because of it.

The Legacy

Years later, when Yaakov's children faced trials of their own, they remembered that shuttered shop on Shabbos. They remembered the hunger in their bellies at times, but also the peace that filled their home. Most of all, they remembered how faith — though the world mocked it as madness — became their family's wellspring of blessing.

Musar Reflection

Hebrew:
האמונה נבחנת דווקא במקום שבו נראה ההפסד לעין. מי שסוגר את חנותו לשבת מגלה שהפרנסה איננה בידיו — אלא ביד ה'.

Translation:
Faith is tested precisely where loss seems most visible. One who closes his shop for Shabbos discovers that livelihood is not in his hands, but in Hashem's.

Takeaway: True faith is not proclaimed with words but lived in deeds — in choices that sacrifice comfort for the sake of truth.

The Physician's Hands: Emunah in Illness (אמונה בחולי)

"Heal us, Hashem, and we shall be healed; save us, and we shall be saved."
(Jeremiah 17:14)

The Diagnosis

In Lemberg lived Baruch, a tailor of simple life. His stitches were precise, his words humble, his faith steady. Then one winter he fell gravely ill. His hands, once quick with needle and thread, trembled; his body burned with fever. Doctors shook their heads. *"Prepare your home,"* they said gently. *"We cannot help."*

The words fell heavy. His wife wept at his bedside, his children clung to her skirts. But Baruch whispered: *"The doctor may hold the knife, but Hashem guides the hand. Until He speaks, I will not despair."*

The Struggle of Night

The nights were hardest. Pain pressed like iron, breath came in gasps. Each time he felt darkness closing in, he forced his lips to murmur Tehillim.

"Hashem," he prayed, *"if You heal me, I will sing louder than before. And if You do not — still I will trust You."*

His family, hearing his whispers, drew strength from his words. The house became less a chamber of fear, more a sanctuary of faith.

The Unexpected Turn

One dawn, as the fever still raged, a young physician newly arrived in town came to visit. He examined Baruch and prescribed a treatment the older doctors had dismissed as foolish. *"It may not help,"* he admitted, *"but I believe it is worth trying."*

Baruch's wife hesitated. The others had already given up. But Baruch nodded: *"If Hashem sent this doctor to my door, I will receive him as His messenger."*

They followed the treatment. Days passed. Slowly, the fever broke. Color returned to Baruch's face, strength to his limbs. Within weeks, he was again at his sewing bench, the needle flashing in sunlight.

The Song of Thanksgiving

When he returned to the synagogue, the community looked at him as if seeing a man risen from the grave. Baruch lifted his voice in *Nishmat Kol Chai* with such fire that many wept.

Later, he told his children: *"Do not place your trust in doctors alone, nor dismiss them. Trust in the One who sends them. Emunah is knowing that every cure, every failure, every breath comes from Hashem."*

Musar Reflection

Hebrew:
האמונה בחולי איננה עיוורון לרפואה, אלא הבנה שהרופא רק שליח. ההחלטה — בידי רופא כל בשר.

Translation:
Emunah in illness is not blind rejection of medicine, but the understanding that the physician is only a messenger. The final decision rests in the hands of the Healer of all flesh.

Takeaway: Faith means holding Hashem's hand in the valley of illness — whether through doctors, medicine, or miracles.

The Empty Cradle: Emunah Through Tears (אמונה)

"Hope in Hashem, be strong and let your heart take courage, and hope in Hashem."
(Psalms 27:14)

The Pain of Waiting

In a small village near Minsk lived Shlomo and Devorah, a young couple married five years without children. Their home was neat, filled with books and warmth, but one corner always pierced their hearts: the empty cradle by the window.

Neighbors tried to comfort them, but their words often wounded. *"Pray harder,"* some said. Others whispered, *"Perhaps you are not worthy."* The couple smiled politely, but each night their pillows were soaked with tears.

The Choice of Faith

One spring, Shlomo returned from the beit midrash with red eyes. "Devorah," he said, "today the Rav taught: Emunah is not believing when Hashem gives, but when Hashem withholds. I want us to live that truth."

From that night onward, they began inviting orphans to their Shabbat table. They filled the empty cradle with folded clothes and toys to give away. Their home rang with children's laughter — not their own, but laughter nonetheless.

Neighbors wondered: *"Why do they not despair?"* But Shlomo and Devorah answered: *"Hashem has not forgotten us. Until He opens our womb, we will open our door."*

The Long Road

Years passed. Their hair turned gray, their steps slowed. They never stopped praying, but neither did they stop giving. Dozens of children remembered their home as the warmest in the shtetl. Some called Devorah *"Mama Devorah,"* though she had never given birth.

Yet still, in the quiet moments, the cradle by the window ached. Faith does not erase pain, but it gives strength to carry it.

The Unseen Blessing

One winter night, the town caught fire. Flames consumed homes; families fled into the snow. It was Shlomo and Devorah's house — sturdy, always open — that became a refuge. They laid children in the cradle, not their own, but saved from the flames. They fed, clothed, and comforted dozens.

Later, the Rav said: *"Do you see? Hashem gave you children — not one, but many. The cradle was never empty. It was waiting for its true purpose."*

The Legacy of Emunah

Shlomo and Devorah never bore children of their own. Yet when they departed this world, hundreds gathered at their graves, weeping as if for parents. And the words most often whispered were: *"They taught us emunah."*

Musar Reflection

Hebrew:
אמונה איננה מבטיחה תוצאה מסוימת, אלא מחייבת לבטוח שגם היעדר — מלא בתכלית. הקרבן הגדול ביותר יכול להפוך לברכה לאחרים, אם נישא אותו באמונה.

Translation:
Emunah does not guarantee the outcome we desire. It calls us to trust that even absence is filled with purpose. The greatest sacrifice can become a blessing for others, if borne with faith.

Takeaway: Faith is not measured by what we receive, but by how we live when our prayers seem unanswered.

The Last Coin: Emunah in Livelihood (אמונה בפרנסה)

"You open Your hand and satisfy the desire of every living thing."
(Psalms 145:16)

The Final Kopeck

Reb Herschel, a peddler in Minsk, had fallen on hard times. Winter bit deeply, and business was as frozen as the rivers. One morning he checked his pocket and found only a single coin — one kopeck. His cupboard was bare; his children shivered in rags.

His wife looked at him with weary eyes. *"Herschel, spend it wisely. At least we need bread."*

Herschel nodded. But inside, a storm raged: *This coin is my last anchor. Should I cling to it — or release it into Hashem's hand?*

The Test of the Tzedakah Box

As he walked through the market, he passed the synagogue. At the door stood a small wooden *pushke*, its slot worn smooth by generations of coins. Herschel stopped. The coin in his pocket weighed heavy as iron.

One voice within him cried: *Fool! Keep it for your children.*
Another whispered: *Trust Hashem. What you give for His sake is never lost.*

With trembling fingers, he dropped the coin into the box. The hollow clink echoed louder than all the cries of the market. His pocket was empty — but his heart felt strangely light.

The Hidden Return

That afternoon, as Herschel trudged home, a carriage wheel splashed mud over his boots. The wealthy merchant inside leaned out, apologetic: *"Good man, your boots are ruined! Come to my shop tomorrow; I will pay you for new leather and for making me a pair."*

True to his word, the merchant hired him not just for one job but for steady work. Within weeks, Herschel's home was filled with food, and his children's cheeks glowed with health.

When his wife asked how the turn began, he pointed to the little *pushke* by the synagogue door.

The Lesson Carried

From then on, Herschel set aside a coin from every profit, however small. His children learned early: *Parnassah is not in the kopeck you hold, but in the hand of Hashem.*

And in later years, when they told the story of their father's good fortune, they never mentioned the merchant or the boots. They said only: *"It began with the last coin, given with emunah."*

Musar Reflection

Hebrew:
הפרנסה איננה מן הכיס אלא מן השמים. דווקא כאשר האדם נותן את המעט שיש לו, נפתחים שערי ברכה.

Translation:
Livelihood comes not from the pocket but from Heaven. Precisely when a person gives from the little he has, the gates of blessing open.

Takeaway: The strongest emunah in livelihood is not shown when we give from abundance, but when we trust Hashem enough to give from our very last coin.

The Road to Nowhere: Emunah in Exile (אמונה בגלות)

"For Hashem will not abandon His people."
(Psalms 94:14)

The Expulsion

In the year 1492, when Jews were expelled from Spain, families poured onto the roads, their wagons piled high with the little they could carry. Among them walked Reb Eliyahu, an elderly *melamed*, leading his grandchildren by the hand. His beard was white, his back bent, but his eyes shone with something unbroken.

The roads were heavy with sorrow. Some wept, others cursed, and still others muttered bitterly: *"Hashem has forsaken us. Where is His promise?"*

But Reb Eliyahu whispered Tehillim as they trudged along; each verse became a step, each step a quiet defiance of despair.

The Night of Hunger

One evening, after days of travel, they stopped in a barren field. Their food was gone. The children whimpered from hunger; even the strongest men sat silent, staring into the dust.

A neighbor cried out: *"Rabbi, what now? We are abandoned, betrayed!"*

Reb Eliyahu gathered the children close and said: *"Children, remember this: a Jew without bread can survive. A Jew without emunah cannot."*

He lifted his hands to heaven and softly sang: *"Ani ma'amin — I believe with complete faith."* Slowly, other voices joined, until the entire field rang with song. Hunger remained, but despair fled.

The Hidden Hand

That night, as the camp slept, riders approached. Fear seized the exiles — but it was only a band of traders who had lost their way. Seeing the starving wanderers, they opened their packs and gave bread and dried fruit.

"Why share with us?" they asked.

The leader shrugged. *"We meant to sell this in the next town, but a strange pull led us here instead. Perhaps Hashem willed it so."*

Reb Eliyahu smiled through tears. *"You are His messengers. He has not forgotten His people."*

The Journey Continues

The exiles reached the port and sailed to new lands. Many carried scars of loss. But in every new community, the story was told: how in the darkest night, faith lit their path and bread arrived as if from heaven.

Reb Eliyahu lived only a few more years, but his grandchildren remembered his voice: *"A Jew without bread can survive. A Jew without emunah cannot."* They taught it to their children, who taught it to theirs, until it became the heartbeat of a wandering nation — beaten, but never broken.

Musar Reflection

Hebrew:
בגלות ובאובדן, האדם עלול לחשוב שנעזב. אך האמונה מלמדת שגם בדרך לא ידועה, השגחת ה׳ הולכת לפנינו.

Translation:
In exile and in loss, one might think he has been abandoned. But emunah teaches that even on the road to nowhere, Hashem's providence walks ahead of us.

Takeaway: Exile tests the body, but faith sustains the soul. A Jew who carries emunah is never truly homeless.

The Bridge of Faith: Emunah at the Crossing (אמונה במעבר)

"When you pass through the waters, I am with you; and through the rivers, they shall not overwhelm you."
 (Isaiah 43:2)

The Crossing

In a mountain village of Eastern Europe, a wooden bridge spanned a raging river. Traders feared it, for the planks were rotten and the current below devoured anything that fell. Yet the bridge was the only path to the market.

Reb Yitzchak, a teacher with barely enough to feed his family, needed to cross. His sack of books weighed on his back, and the hungry faces of his children pressed upon his heart. At the bridge's edge, the merchants hesitated, whispering of danger. Yitzchak whispered Tehillim.

The Fear

As he stepped onto the creaking planks, fear clutched him. Each groan of wood seemed to mock his faith. Halfway across, the wind rose, the river roared louder, and panic nearly drove him back.

But then he remembered his father's words: *"When Hashem calls you to cross, the bridge is stronger than it looks. Do not see the water — see the Hand that holds you above it."*

Yitzchak closed his eyes, gripped the ropes, and sang softly: *"Hashem li, lo ira"* — *"Hashem is with me, I shall not fear."*

The Step of Emunah

With each step, his song grew louder. Other travelers, frozen at the edge, heard him and found courage. One by one they followed, their voices joining his. The bridge still shook, but fear no longer ruled.

When they reached the far bank, the traders embraced him. *"It was your voice that carried us, not the planks."*

Yitzchak shook his head: *"No. It was Hashem's hand. I only reminded you it was there."*

The Lesson for His Students

That evening in the *cheder*, Yitzchak told his pupils: *"Life is many bridges. Some are sturdy, some rotten. Do not measure their strength with your eyes, but with your emunah. The river rages to frighten, but Hashem carries us across."*

Years later, his students, grown into men, remembered their teacher's story whenever they faced their own crossings. And they, too, whispered: *"Hashem li, lo ira."*

Musar Reflection

Hebrew:
.כל גשר בחיים נראה רעוע, אך מי שמביט ביד ה' ולא במים הזועפים – עובר בשלום

Translation:
Every bridge in life seems fragile, but one who looks to Hashem's hand and not at the raging waters passes in peace.

Takeaway: Faith does not silence the roar of the river — it gives us the strength to walk across it.

The Soldier's Psalm: Emunah in Danger (אמונה בסכנה)

"If you walk in My statutes... I will grant peace in the land."
(Leviticus 26:3,6)

The Eve of Battle

It was night. The sky hung heavy over the army camp, and the air trembled with tension. A young Jewish soldier sat on his backpack, hands clasped around a small, worn *Tehillim* he had carried since his bar mitzvah. His mother had given him the booklet with tears in her eyes:

"My son," she had said, "you may go to places where I cannot protect you. But this little book—these are the words that have always protected our people. Hold it. Sing from it. Speak from it. Then you are never alone."

Now, in the middle of the camp, he heard the bustle of soldiers, the tapping of metal tools, the click of rifles being loaded. But in his mind, only his mother's voice sounded.

The Silence Before the Storm

When the first artillery boomed, the ground itself seemed to shudder. He crawled into a trench, pressed his back to the earth, and felt fear surge through his body. "Where is the peace the Torah promises?" he whispered. "*If you walk in My statutes... I will give peace.*" His mind said: "Look around you—bullets, smoke, terror. Where is peace here?" But his heart said: "Perhaps peace is not outside you, but within you."

The Voice of *Tehillim*

He opened his *Tehillim*, almost instinctively to Psalm 23:

"*Gam ki elech b'gei tzalmavet, lo ira ra, ki Atah imadi.*"
"Even though I walk through the valley of deep darkness, I will fear no evil, for You are with me."

These words no longer came from the mouth of a child in a safe shul. They came from his throat, hoarse, tears in his eyes, as shells exploded around him. And with every letter, his heart seemed to build a wall of strength.

A Dialogue of Fear and Faith

He closed his eyes for a moment and seemed to hear two voices within himself.

The voice of fear said:
"You are lost. No one can save you here. This is the end."

The voice of *emunah* answered:
"I am never alone. My people have stood in darkness for centuries—Egypt, Babylonia, Spain, Auschwitz. Yet I live. Yet I sing. If they could survive through faith, so can I."

He thought of his rebbe, who always said: "*Emunah* is not a luxury. It is the weapon you carry when everything else is taken from you."

A Lesson from His Father

Suddenly he remembered an evening at home. His father had taken him to shul, and on the way had told him:

"Son, do you know why the Torah says, 'I will give peace in the land'? Because peace is not a given. It is a gift from Hashem. But to receive that gift, a person must learn to carry peace within himself. For one who knows no peace in his heart will never find it in the world."

Those words returned now, like a light in the darkness.

Dawn

The night seemed endless, but at last a pale glow appeared on the horizon. The shooting eased, the smoke slowly lifted. The soldier looked up and saw the first sunlight breaking through the clouds. His body was exhausted, his uniform torn, but his soul felt lighter than ever.

He pressed the *Tehillim* to his lips and whispered:
"Hashem, You have taught me that peace does not mean there is no war. Peace is that even in war, my heart finds rest in You."

Epilogue: A Psalm Engraved on the Heart

Years later, when he was safely home, he told this story to his children. He showed them the little *Tehillim*, its edges still blackened from that night."This booklet," he said, "was my shield. Not against bullets, but against despair. Remember, children: peace does not begin with treaties or armies. Peace begins with *emunah*—with the trust that Hashem is with you, wherever you go."And so the soldier's psalm remained not only a memory of a dangerous night, but a lesson for all generations:
Even in the valley of the shadow of death, *emunah* can fill the heart with peace.

The Soldier's Psalm: Emunah in Danger (אמונה בסכנה)

"If you walk in My statutes… then I will grant peace in the land."
(Vayikra / Leviticus 26:3,6)

The Eve of Battle

It was night. The sky hung heavy over the army camp, and the air trembled with tension. A young Jewish soldier sat on his backpack, his hands clasped around a small, worn *Tehillim* he had carried since his bar mitzvah. His mother had given it to him with tears in her eyes:

"My son," she had said, *"you may go to places where I cannot protect you. But this little book—these are the words that have always protected our people. Hold it close. Sing from it. Speak from it. Then you will never be alone."*

Now, in the middle of the camp, he heard the rumble of soldiers, the clinking of tools, the clicking of rifles being loaded. But in his mind he heard only his mother's voice.

The Silence Before the Storm

When the first artillery thundered, the ground itself seemed to shudder. He crawled into a trench, pressed his back against the earth, and felt fear racing through his body.

"Where is the peace that the Torah promises?" he whispered. *"If you walk in My statutes... I will grant peace."*

His reason said: *"Look around you—bullets, smoke, terror. Where is peace here?"*
But his heart said: *"Perhaps peace is not outside of you, but within you."*

The Voice of Tehillim

He opened his *Tehillim*—almost instinctively—to Psalm 23:

"Gam ki elech b'gei tzalmavet, lo ira ra, ki Atah imadi."
"Even though I walk through the valley of deepest darkness, I will fear no evil, for You are with me."

The words no longer came from the mouth of a child in a safe shul. They came hoarse, with tears in his eyes, while shells exploded around him. And with every letter, his heart seemed to build a wall of strength.

A Dialogue of Fear and Faith

He closed his eyes for a moment and heard, as if within himself, two voices.

The voice of fear said:
"You are lost. No one can save you here. This is the end."

The voice of *emunah* replied:
"I am never alone. My people have stood in darkness for centuries—Egypt, Babylon, Spain, Auschwitz. Yet I live. Yet I sing. If they could survive through faith, so can I."

He thought of his *rebbe*, who always said:
"Emunah is not a luxury. It is the weapon you carry when everything else is taken from you."

A Lesson From His Father

Suddenly he remembered one evening at home. His father had taken him to shul, and on the way had said:

"Son, do you know why the Torah says: 'I will grant peace in the land'? Because peace is not guaranteed. It is a gift from Hashem. But to receive that gift, a man must first learn to carry peace within himself. For one who has no peace in his heart will never find it in the world."

Those words now returned, a light in the darkness.

The Dawn

The night seemed endless, but at last a pale glow spread along the horizon. The gunfire slowed, the smoke began to lift. The soldier looked up and saw the first sunlight breaking through the clouds. His body was exhausted, his uniform torn, but his soul felt lighter than ever.

He pressed the *Tehillim* to his lips and whispered:
"Hashem, You have taught me that peace does not mean the absence of war. Peace means that even in war, my heart finds rest in You."

Epilogue: A Psalm Engraved in the Heart

Years later, when he was safely home, he told this story to his children. He showed them the little *Tehillim*, still blackened at the edges from that night.

"This book," he said, *"was my shield. Not against bullets, but against despair. Remember, children: peace does not begin with treaties or armies. Peace begins with emunah—with trusting that Hashem is with you, wherever you go."*

And so the soldier's psalm remained not only a memory of a dangerous night, but a lesson for all generations:
Even in the valley of the shadow of death, *emunah* can fill the heart with peace.

The Lone Soldier — Arrelle's Sacrifice

Risen from the Ashes

He was still very young when he left the gates of hell behind. The camps had taken everything from him: his parents, his brothers and sisters, his town, his youth. When he was finally liberated, he found himself alone in the world. No home, no family, no future—only the memories that kept him awake at night.

Even so, he decided: **I will live.** And when the news came that a Jewish state would be born, that there would be a land where the Jewish people could defend themselves, he knew where he had to go. He set out for **Eretz Yisrael**—exhausted, broken, but with a spark in his heart: **hope**.

In Uniform

They put a rifle in his hands, a uniform far too big for him, and a command in Hebrew he barely understood. He still spoke Yiddish and Polish, but the language of war he had heard too often: orders, shouting, the smell of gunpowder.

And yet, this felt different. Here he did not fight to **survive**, but to **build**. This was not a war of destruction, but of rebuilding. The army gave him a name: **chayal boded**—a lone soldier. But he did not feel alone, because he fought for his people, for a future in which the children of Jerusalem could laugh without fear.

Camaraderie

In his loneliness he found a friend. His name was **Arrelle**—a boy from Jaffa, raised by the sea, with dark eyes that always sparkled with life. They could hardly speak to each other—one spoke broken Hebrew, the other only a little Yiddish—but they understood each other without words. They shared bread, shared fear, and sometimes, for a brief moment, shared dreams.

Arrelle often said:

"Listen, brother: you survived the camps. You **must** live. You have to show the world that not all of us died. If even one of us remains to bear witness, it will have been worth it."

The survivor smiled faintly, his eyes filling with tears. He knew Arrelle was right.

The Battle

One day, in a bloody battle around **Latrun**, they charged forward together. Bullets hissed around them; the air was thick with smoke and screams. The lone soldier felt his body stiffen with fear—he had lived this before in Europe, but this time there was a difference: he was not fighting for a camp commandant; **he was fighting for his people**.

Suddenly a shot rang out—sharp, close. The bullet was meant for him. But in a fraction of a second, Arrelle leapt in front. He **took** the bullet in his chest.

The lone soldier screamed his name, but the roar of battle swallowed his voice. He knelt beside him as the blood darkened the earth.

Arrelle looked at him, his eyes still bright, and whispered with his last breath:

"Live... live for both of us. You must tell the story."

And then came silence.

A Soldier and a Psalm

After the battle, the lone soldier stood alone, rifle in hand and a **Tehillim** in his breast pocket. He opened it and read in a trembling voice:

"Lo amut ki echye, va'asaper ma'aseh Kah."
"I shall not die but live, and declare the works of Hashem." (Psalm 118:17)

Those words became his vow. **He would live.** Not only for himself, but also for Arrelle, for all who had fallen in the camps and on the battlefield.

Epilogue

Years later, sitting in his home in a flourishing Israeli city, he told the story to his grandchildren. He pointed to the photo on the wall—a young man with dark eyes and an eternal smile.

"This is **Arrelle**," he said softly. "He gave his life so that I could continue mine. Never forget his name. Thanks to him I live—and thanks to him, **you** do too."

And in that room, filled with children and grandchildren, it was clear: Arrelle's sacrifice had borne fruit. **The Jewish people lived.**

IN SIX DAYS THE WORLD CHANGED FOREVER

Part I – Before the Storm

The soldier's name was Avi Shalev. He was twenty-one, born in the years of hope and fear that shaped the new State of Israel. His parents had survived the devastation of Europe and had arrived in Haifa with only a suitcase and their unshakable faith that the land of their ancestors would give them new life.

Avi grew up in a modest apartment above a grocery store, where the walls held the scent of oranges and sea salt from the nearby port. Life in Israel in the early 1960s was not easy, but Avi remembered it as a time of determination. His mother patched his shirts with the same hands that had once carried heavy stones in a refugee camp. His father, who rarely spoke of his youth, kept a siddur by his bedside, and each night whispered the Shema into the silence.

From his father, Avi learned that faith was not made of words but of perseverance. From his mother, he learned that love was an act of building: cooking one more meal, sweeping one more floor, even when the body ached.

When Avi was called to the IDF, his parents stood proudly. His father embraced him with tears in his eyes and said only:

"You are my answer to Pharaoh, to Amalek, to all who said we would vanish."

Rumors of War

In 1967, Avi was a paratrooper, stationed near the Judean hills. News spread quickly that spring: Egypt was moving troops into the Sinai, Syria threatened from the north, and Jordan was making vengeful speeches. The air in the kibbutzim and towns was heavy with tension. Radios blared with updates, and mothers whispered in markets: *Will this be the end?*

Avi wrote letters to his parents, careful not to frighten them. "Don't worry," he scrawled in his uneven handwriting. "We are strong. Hashem is with us. And we stand together as brothers."

But at night, lying on the rough army cot, he admitted to himself that he was afraid. The numbers were grim. Israel had fewer planes, fewer tanks, fewer men. Their enemies had sworn to drive them into the sea. The young country was only nineteen years old—barely more than a dream—and now it seemed that dream might be extinguished.

The Waiting

By late May, the soldiers were confined to their bases. Days turned into weeks. Avi and his unit trained, cleaned their weapons, checked their parachutes again and again. But the heaviest burden was not the weapons, but the silence. The waiting.

In those days, Avi often thought of Jerusalem. He had never truly seen her. He had been to the modern western neighborhoods—the cafés, the narrow streets—but the Old City lay beyond the border, in Jordanian hands since 1948. He had heard of the Kotel, the last remnant of the Beit HaMikdash, but only from books, from whispered stories of pilgrims and grandfathers. To him, it was almost mythical: a wall of stone that had heard the cries of a thousand years, a wall that had waited for a people scattered and now returning.

When he prayed with the other soldiers, he imagined those stones. He wondered what it would be like to press his palm against them, to whisper the Shema into their ancient cracks.

One night, as the men tried to sleep, one of the older reservists, Moshe, began softly humming a melody. It was the song *Yerushalayim Shel Zahav*, Naomi Shemer's new hymn. The words floated gently in the darkness: *"The city that sits alone, and in its heart—a wall."*

Avi shivered. He whispered to himself: "Will I ever see it?"

Farewell

On June 4th, the orders came. War was no longer a question of *if*, but of *when*. Avi was given twenty-four hours of leave to see his parents. He took the bus to Haifa. The streets were quieter than he remembered; even the children seemed subdued, as if they too understood the weight of the moment.

His mother had filled the table with food, though she hardly ate. She sat across from him, studying his face as if she wanted to etch it into memory.
"You will come back," she said firmly, though her voice trembled. "Remember, you carry generations with you."

His father walked him to the door. They stood for a long time without words. Then his father placed his hands on Avi's head, like a kohen giving a blessing.
"May Hashem guard your going out and your coming in. And if you see the Kotel," he whispered, "kiss it for me as well."

The Morning of War

At dawn on June 5th, sirens shattered the silence. The war had begun. Egyptian planes were destroyed on the ground in a lightning strike, and soon the fighting spread to every front. Avi's unit was moved toward the center—Jerusalem was calling.

The ride was tense, filled with dust and the smell of sweat and oil. Tanks thundered along the roads, soldiers shouted to one another, jeeps sped by with orders. Avi clutched his rifle, his knuckles white.

Jerusalem. He did not yet know if he would live to see her, or if she would be the last sight his eyes would behold.

But in his heart he carried his father's blessing, his mother's gaze, and something older than both: the memory of a people who had always dreamed of returning.

And so, the paratroopers advanced, into the storm of history.

Part II – The Battle for Jerusalem

The City Within

The thunder of artillery filled the air as Avi's unit approached Jerusalem. The hills surrounding the city were strewn with bunkers, barbed wire, and Jordanian snipers who knew the terrain well. For nineteen years the Old City had been closed off, and now the paratroopers were given the impossible order: break through and return to the heart of the Jewish people.

The trucks stopped at the Mandelbaum Gate. Avi jumped down, his boots landing with a dull thud on the dusty road. Around him, men adjusted their helmets, checked their rifles, tightened their belts. The command moved down the line: forward.

Every corner was a threat. The Jordanians had fortified every alley and rooftop. As Avi's group advanced, bullets ricocheted off the walls, and dust rained down. They ran crouched, close to the stone houses, their breaths short, their hearts pounding.

Moshe, the older reservist, whispered hoarsely:
"Stay close together, boys. Don't forget—this is not just war. This is Yerushalayim."

Ammunition Hill

The fiercest battle took place at Givat HaTachmoshet—Ammunition Hill. The Jordanians had built a complex network of bunkers and trenches, manned by elite troops. Capturing this hill was the key to opening the road to the Old City.

At midnight, Avi's unit received the order: storm the hill. Darkness surrounded them as they moved up, but flares lit the sky and turned night into day. Machine-gun fire erupted, bullets whizzing past their helmets. Men fell, screaming, bleeding.

Avi threw himself into a trench and landed hard on his shoulder. A Jordanian soldier lunged at him with a bayonet. Avi's rifle jammed; panic surged through him. But instinct took over—he struck with the butt of his weapon and knocked the enemy back. Gunfire cracked beside him as another paratrooper, Yossi, covered him.

"Move, Avi!" Yossi shouted, sweat streaming down his face.

They pushed forward, grenade after grenade, trench after trench. The ground shook, their ears rang from the blasts. The smell of gunpowder and blood mixed with the damp earth. For hours they fought man to man, crawling, shooting, praying.

At dawn, silence fell. Ammunition Hill was theirs, but at a terrible price. Dozens of comrades lay still behind. Avi slumped against a sandbag wall, his hands trembling as he lit a cigarette from a fallen officer's pack. He had no words—only the realization that every life lost was part of something greater.

The Order to Advance

The next day, June 7, came the command: "Paratroopers, forward to the Old City."

The men could hardly believe it. Avi felt his chest tighten. The Old City—that labyrinth of stone, closed off since '48, forbidden to Jews. His father had spoken of it with reverence, as if it were another world. And now, exhausted and battered, they were ordered to reclaim it.

The unit moved through the narrow streets of East Jerusalem. The sound of gunfire echoed off the walls, mingling with the imagined echoes of prayers that still clung to the stones. Avi looked up and saw the golden dome gleaming in the morning sun. Behind it, hidden yet near, lay the Kotel.

The Lions' Gate

Their entry point was Sha'ar HaArayot—the Lions' Gate. Tanks screeched to a halt; the paratroopers leapt out, rifles raised. Avi's boots struck the cobblestones as they stormed through the ancient gate, bullets ricocheting off the walls.

"Kadima!" shouted their commander, Motta Gur. "Forward!"

Through twisting alleys they ran, gunfire crackling behind them. Avi's heart pounded, not only with fear but with awe. Every stone seemed alive, whispering: *We have been waiting for you.*

They reached the Via Dolorosa. Doors slammed shut, windows closed as they advanced. Dust swirled around them, mingled with the acrid smoke of explosives. Every corner could hide an enemy, every rooftop a sniper.

And yet Avi felt, as they pressed deeper, something greater than fear. As if unseen hands were pushing them forward, carrying their weary legs, steadying their aim.

Sacrifice and Courage

Near the Church of St. Anne, a sudden burst of fire cut through their column. Avi dove behind a stone wall. Yossi, the one who had saved him on Ammunition Hill, groaned and collapsed. Avi crawled to him and pulled him back. Blood stained his uniform red.

"Go," Yossi gasped, clutching Avi's sleeve. "Don't stay for me. Yerushalayim… waits."

Avi's throat tightened. He pressed Yossi's hand and whispered the Shema in his ear. Then he rose, heavy with grief, and moved on, each step a promise to carry Yossi's words.

Toward the Temple Mount

The sounds of battle began to fade. Rumors spread along the line: the Jordanians were retreating. The Old City was opening before them. Avi's chest burned with exhaustion, but he felt pulled forward by an invisible cord.

Suddenly the column turned a corner—and there it was. The Temple Mount lay before them, vast and golden under the blazing sun. And behind it, hidden but close, the Wall awaited.

Avi stood still, breathless. He had dreamed of this moment in whispered prayers, in childhood stories, in his father's trembling voice. Now it was real.

The voice of their commander rang through the radio, words that would echo through history:
"Har HaBayit beyadeinu! The Temple Mount is in our hands!"

The men shouted, wept, embraced. Avi wiped dust and sweat from his face, his heart soaring. But he knew: this was not yet the end. He had to see it himself. He had to touch the stones that had waited for centuries, silent but faithful.

The Kotel was near.

Part III – At the Kotel

The Gate to the Heart

The sun stood high as the paratroopers made their way through the narrow alleys. Each step echoed against ancient stones, soaked with stories and tears. Avi felt his legs heavy, but his soul light. He knew he was walking toward the heart of his people.

The sounds of battle faded. Here and there they still heard an occasional shot, but the Old City was practically in their hands. The radio crackled: "The area is secure. Forward to the Kotel."

Avi's breath caught. He felt his heart beating faster. The Kotel. The Wall. The last witness of the House we had lost.

The First Sight

They turned a corner and entered an open square. And there, for the first time in his life, Avi saw it: the Kotel.

Tall, majestic, full of cracks in which thousands of notes and prayers had been placed over the centuries. Birds circled above the stones, as if they were guardians who had never left.

Avi could not look away. He walked slowly, as if his feet themselves hesitated. As he came closer, his eyes filled with tears. *This is it. This is what my father dreamed of, what my mother prayed for, what generations longed for.*

Around him, soldiers burst into tears. Some fell to their knees, others pressed their hands against the Wall and sobbed aloud. An officer blew a shofar; the sound cut through the air, raw and powerful, as if the soul of the nation itself answered across the centuries.

Avi's Touch

At last, Avi stood directly before the stones. He reached out his hand. His fingers trembled as they touched the cool, rough wall. He pressed his forehead against it, closed his eyes, and whispered:

"Lo amut ki echye, va'asaper ma'aseh Kah. I shall not die but live, and declare the deeds of Hashem."

He thought of Yossi, who had fallen, of the boys who would never return. He thought of his father who had said: *"And when you see the Kotel, kiss it for me too."*

Avi kissed the stone. "Abba," he whispered, "this is for you."

A Prayer from Centuries

The silence that followed was no ordinary silence. It was as if he could hear the voices of centuries. The whispers of Jews from Spain, from Poland, from Yemen, who had all left their tears in these stones.

He no longer felt like a young soldier, sweaty and exhausted. He was part of something infinitely greater: a chain of souls that had never been broken.

A rabbi who had joined the soldiers lifted his voice:
"Baruch ata Hashem, shehecheyanu, vekiyemanu, vehigiyanu lazman hazeh."

Together the soldiers answered "Amen," their voices cracked with emotion.

Notes in the Cracks

Avi pulled from his breast pocket a small note he had written during the days of waiting. Just a few words:

"Grant peace to my people. Give strength to my parents. Forgive me if I do not return."

With trembling fingers, he placed it between the stones. Then he leaned forward again and felt a deep peace descend upon him. For the first time in weeks, he exhaled fully.

Brothers at the Wall

Soldiers stood side by side, arms around each other's shoulders. Some softly sang *Ani Ma'amin*, others whispered psalms. Some remained silent, but their tears spoke.

Moshe, the reservist who had often sung, placed his hand on Avi's shoulder. "Do you know what this means, boy? We are the first generation in two thousand years to stand here not as strangers, but as liberators."

Avi nodded, but could not speak. His throat was tight.

The Oath

That afternoon, as the sun cast its golden light upon the Wall, Avi sealed an oath in his heart. He would live. Not only for himself, but for Yossi, for all the fallen, for his parents, and for the generations who had never been able to see this moment.

He would tell their story. He would testify that the dream had not died. That a wall of stone, old and cracked, had once again welcomed the heart of a living people.

Part IV – Epilogue and Legacy

Years Later

Many years passed since those six days that changed the course of history. Avi Shalev grew older, had children, and eventually grandchildren. The soldier's uniform had long since stopped hanging by the door; instead, he wore glasses, walked more slowly, and smiled more often. Yet in his heart he always carried the scent of dust and gunpowder, the sound of sirens, and above all, the image of the Kotel on that day he first saw it.

He lived in a thriving city in Israel, surrounded by the sounds of children playing, the bustle of markets, and the life of a people reborn. Sometimes he sat in his living room and looked at the photos on the wall — photos of young soldiers, of his parents, and of the day he laid his hand upon those ancient stones.

Telling the Story

On Shabbat afternoons his grandchildren often called out: "Zeide, tell us again about the war. Tell us about Jerusalem."

Avi smiled and settled into his chair, while the children plopped down on the floor around him. He took a deep breath and began his story once more: about the fear in the spring of 1967, the silence on the bases, the battle on Ammunition Hill, the Lions' Gate, and finally, the Wall.

He described how the stones felt cold and rough under his hand, how the tears would not stop, how the shofar sounded as if heaven itself sang along. The children listened breathlessly, their eyes wide, as if through his words they could see that day anew.

The Name That Does Not Disappear

On Avi's living room wall hung a framed photo. It was not of himself, but of Yossi, his comrade who had fallen in the streets of Jerusalem. Every time he told the story, Avi pointed to the photo.

"This is Yossi," he said softly. "He saved my life, and gave his own so that we could reach the Wall. Never forget his name. For every time I touch the Kotel, I carry his memory with me as well."

His grandchildren nodded solemnly. For them, Yossi was not a distant figure from a history book, but someone who was part of their family, of their very existence.

A Living Testimony

One day Avi brought his whole family to Jerusalem. Together they walked through the narrow alleys of the Old City, along the same stones where he had once run with his weapon. He held the smallest hands of his grandchildren, and his eyes filled with tears once again.

When they reached the plaza by the Kotel, Avi stopped. He let the children run ahead, watching as they placed their tiny hands on the wall, whispered, and laughed.

He walked slowly forward himself, placed his hand once more on the same stone he had kissed decades earlier, and whispered:
"Thank You, Hashem. You brought us back. You let me live."

The Legacy

That evening, back in his home, Avi wrote in his journal:
"We were young and afraid. We fought because we had to, but also because we believed. The world thought we would not survive. Yet here we are. The Kotel no longer stands alone. The Jewish people live, and my children and grandchildren are my proof."

He closed the book, blew out the candles, and smiled. For he knew: the wall of stone had absorbed his story, and would continue to whisper it through the generations.

Conclusion

The echo of the shofar that day remained in Avi's soul until his last breath. And each time new generations place their hands upon the Kotel, they silently repeat the same words he first whispered there:

"Lo amut ki echye, va'asaper ma'aseh Kah — I shall not die but live, and declare the deeds of Hashem."

Thus Avi's life became not only that of a soldier who survived a war, but of a witness — a living bridge between past and future.

And in that future, in the laughter of his grandchildren and in the singing of songs by the Wall, lay the answer to all fear and all sacrifice:

The Jewish people live.

The Yeshiva in Crisis

It was a tense afternoon in Bnei Brak. Rumors spread quickly that the authorities were arresting Bnei Yeshiva for not reporting to the army. Fear gripped the Beis Midrash.

The Rosh Yeshiva, brokenhearted by the cries of his students, decided to call a respected Rabbi and Dayan in New York—Rabbi David Zvi Vandewaald, known for his think tank and for offering clear vision in times of crisis.

His voice shook as he spoke into the phone:

"Rabbi, we are trembling here in Bnei Brak. The army is arresting bochurim left and right. What should we do?"

The Rabbi's Surprising Counsel

Rabbi Vandewald paused in thought. Then, with calm certainty, he said words that nearly made the Rosh Yeshiva drop the receiver:

"Well, give them what they want. They want Bnei Torah in the army—so give them Bnei Torah in the army."

The Rosh Yeshiva was stunned. "Rabbi, you want us to leave our Batei Midrash, our Torah, and send our bochurim into the army?!"

Rabbi Vandewald replied gently:

"No. Israel is not built on tanks and planes alone. Israel is built on Nissim v'Niflaos—miracles and wonders. And the only way the soldiers will truly be zocheh to win and to have hatzlacha is through Torah."

A Vision of Unity

Rabbi Vandewald continued:

"For the non-religious, it seems unfair. They see young men in the streets during the day, maybe even in restaurants with their wives for anniversaries, while their own sons and daughters are serving in uniform. So the fair thing is—give them what they want.

Tell them: take the entire yeshiva of Bnei Brak, with its thousand boys, and move it into an army base or an air force hangar. Let them continue their Torah studies there. Let them wear a modified army uniform, perhaps with symbols of Torah upon it. They will rise when the soldiers rise, but instead of drills they will go to the Beis Midrash. They will pray, they will learn, they will say Tehillim. And they will not leave until the soldiers go home."

His voice grew stronger:

"In this way, every soldier will have a learning partner—a Ben Torah standing spiritually beside him. One marches with a rifle, the other marches with a Gemara. One fights on the battlefield, the other on the battlefield of Torah. This is the true Yissachar–Zevulun partnership."

Raising the Standards

"Who knows?" the Rabbi added. "Perhaps through this, even the standards in the army will rise. With bochurim in the camps, the kitchens may become more kosher, mashgichim may be appointed, and the atmosphere itself may change.

After all, the Torah itself commands self-defense. Habba b'machteres—hareihu rodef. One who tunnels into your home is a pursuer, and it is a mitzvah to stop him.

This is not abandoning Torah—it is Torah itself that commands us to defend Am Yisrael."

A New Peace Within

So letters were drafted to the army. Slowly, the tension between the religious and non-religious began to soften.

Three months later, an entire Beis Midrash was transferred to a military camp. The sight was unforgettable. Side by side, soldiers in uniform marched with weapons—while others, also in uniform, marched with Gemaras.

The inner conflict of Israel quieted. No longer did one side accuse the other. Both were present in the army camps. Both were serving Am Yisrael.

And when the battles came—from Gaza, from enemies beyond—the miracle was clear. Torah and weapon together brought victory.

The Rabbi's Hope

When Rabbi Vandewald heard the news, he said softly to the Rosh Yeshiva:

"May we be zocheh to see the coming of Moshiach soon. For only when Torah and unity stand together, will Israel truly be at peace."

And thus, a base filled with Torah marched proudly in uniform—Gemara in hand, lips whispering Tehillim—a living testimony that Am Yisrael's strength lies in both faith and action, together as one.

The Candle in the Storm: Holding Fast to Faith (*Emuna*)

"Though I walk through the valley of the shadow of death, I will fear no evil, for You are with me."
(Psalm 23:4)

The Storm

The shtetl of Brisk lay shrouded in storm. Rain lashed the streets, thunder shook the windows, and the river, swollen and furious, threatened to spill over its banks. In a small wooden house on the edge of the village, Chana sat with her children, huddled close around a single flickering candle.

Her husband, a poor wagon driver, had not returned from his journey. Days passed without a word. Every crash of thunder sounded to her like a mocking laugh from heaven at her loneliness.

The children whispered:
—"Mama, will Papa come back?"
She pulled them close, her heart breaking, but answered softly:
—"Yes, your father is in the hands of the Eternal."

Yet deep inside, a painful thought gnawed at her: *What if he is lost? What if my words are only lies?*

The Visit

In the midst of the storm came a knock at the door. A neighbor stepped in, soaked to the bone.

"Chana, forgive me," he said gently, "but in town they say your husband is gone. Two days ago the river swept away a wagon. You should prepare yourself."

The candle flickered weakly. The children clung even closer to her.

Chana closed her eyes. A thousand fears pressed upon her heart. Yet she forced her lips to speak:

—"The Eternal gives life. The Eternal preserves life. Even in the midst of the storm — He is with us."

The neighbor sighed and left, shaking his head.

The Long Night

The hours crawled by. The candle gave only sparks of light, while shadows leapt like claws across the walls. Each roll of thunder sounded like mocking laughter against her psalms. Yet again and again she whispered:

—"Shema Yisrael, Hashem Elokeinu, Hashem Echad."

Slowly the children drifted to sleep, comforted by her voice. She remained awake, alone, murmuring psalms against the storm, clinging to the last thread of faith.

The Dawn

At last the morning light began to glimmer. The storm eased into a gentle drizzle. Chana rose, her body aching and stiff, and opened the door.

There he stood — covered in mud but alive, her husband. His eyes red with exhaustion, but his smile wide.

"The bridge collapsed," he explained. "I had to shelter with a farmer until the river calmed. I came back as quickly as I could."

Chana wept in his arms, and the children danced around them like sparks of the candle that had burned all night.

The Light That Remained

Years later, when her sons faced storms of their own — poverty, illness, exile — they remembered that night: their mother's candle, her trembling yet steadfast voice, her unyielding conviction that the Eternal is present even when the storm rages outside.

And they too, in their darkest nights, whispered psalms and carried their mother's faith as a torch with them.

Moral

Hebrew:

Faith is not waiting until the storm has passed, but in the very storm declaring: "You are with me." The candle kindled in the dark continues to burn in the generations that follow.

Translation:

Faith does not mean waiting until the storm subsides; it means crying out in the midst of the storm: "You are with me." The candle lit in the night continues to shine for generations.

Lesson: Faith is not tested in calm waters, but in the ability to hold fast to the candle when the winds howl.

The Yom Kippur War —

Chapter 1 — The Day of Silence

On the morning of Yom Kippur, the streets of Jerusalem held their breath.

Shutters hung half-drawn against the white heat, cats slept in long strips of sunlight, and the old stones seemed to let go of their fever beneath the whisper of prayer. In synagogues across the city, murmurs wove themselves into pleas, into praise. The land was a single flame, delicately balanced.

Avi Cohen, twenty-eight years old, husband, father, tank commander in the 7th Brigade, stood wrapped in his tallit beside his father. The shawl fell like dove's wings over his shoulders. When he whispered *Avinu Malkeinu*, his voice broke—soft, almost grateful—like that of a man who had learned to carry questions for which no answers exist. Behind the mechitza sat Miriam with their little daughter, Tamar, who traced a fingertip over the embossed letters of the *machzor*, as if the golden ink could warm her skin.

He thought of the past year: Tamar's first day at *gan*; the cracked radiator in their small apartment that hissed all winter like a wayward snake; the tank exercises in the summer dust where the Golan stretched like a sleeping beast. He thought of promises: to be patient, to be brave, to come home.

The prayer hall swelled with *Unetaneh Tokef*. "Who by fire, who by water..." The words were both mirror and sword. Avi's fingers clenched the wooden bench as if he could anchor the whole world there, keep it from turning.

The soldier in olive green entered during *Musaf*. No stomping boots. No slamming door. He stopped just inside the threshold, as though unsure whether he had already broken something holy. His lips moved at the rabbi's ear; the rabbi's eyes closed. His gaze swept across the men's section until it found Avi.

"*Tzav shmoneh*," the rabbi said softly, a tremor in his beard. "Emergency call-up."

Miriam's eyes were already on him, wide yet steady. She tucked Tamar's hair behind her ear, kissed her daughter's head, and rose. They met in the narrow aisle beside the women's section.

"I'll come back," he said.
"You'll come back," she replied, and the word lay between them like both a prayer and a pact.

Outside, the sky held that high, white stillness that belongs only to fast days. A child on a tricycle stopped to stare at the green army truck idling at the curb. Further off, a distant siren practiced its single descending tone—then fell silent. Avi climbed into the back, the door slammed shut, and the city slipped away.

In the truck, other men sat together in silence, their folded *tallitot* on their laps like surrendered sails. When the radio crackled, the driver reflexively reached to turn it off, forgetting that this was not Shabbat but something heavier—a day when even breathing carried weight. The truck climbed and dipped, threading itself through the backbone of the land. As they passed a small moshav, families stood along the road, dressed in white and fasting. A woman raised her hand—not exactly a wave, not exactly a blessing—and pressed her fingers to her lips.

At that moment, Avi felt the first hairline crack run through the day.

At 2:00 p.m., as he stepped into uniform at the armored depot, the sky split open with the sound of artillery. Only it wasn't really sound—it was a shift in pressure, the collapsing of distances. It was Egypt crossing the Suez Canal behind a wall of fire. It was Syria rolling a steel fist over the Golan. In the south, the Bar-Lev Line flared like a row of lit matches. In the north, more than a thousand tanks advanced on fewer than two hundred.

The signal operator went pale. "They've hit us on Yom Kippur," he said, as if naming it might make it smaller.

Avi slipped his dog tags over his head and felt their cold kiss on his sternum. He buttoned his shirt, slid his arm into his jacket, and thought—absurdly—of how Miriam would shake it out when he left it damp over the chair. *"You'll mildew the whole house,"* she would tease, grinning. He tucked that memory into his pocket like a talisman and ran toward the tank sheds.

Chapter 2 — First Fire

The Golan in twilight bore the color of old copper. The basalt fields were already exhaling the heat of the day as Avi's company rolled eastward, treads chewing the road, engines droning low, iron psalms. Dust draped everything in the same weary orange: the columns of tanks; the wiry, muscled boys perched on them; the almond trees bending against the wind.

"Shlomo, you're on the gun," said Avi as he dropped into the commander's hatch. "Yitzhak, ammunition—fast hands today. Eyal, keep those distances honest."

"Yes, commander," came the chorus—the practiced rhythm of men who had eaten from the same pot, cursed the same instructors, learned each other's bad jokes and better habits. Eyal tapped the rangefinder with a knuckle. "Honest enough," he muttered.

The first shells found them as they crested a low ridge. Light tore the dusk open a hundred meters to their left—an impact blooming white at the center, earth exploding upward like joyless fireworks. Shlomo swore softly; Avi did not correct him. He bent to his periscope.

"Column at one o'clock," said Eyal. "Range: twelve-fifty."
"Identify," ordered Avi, though his body already knew. The silhouettes were unmistakable—serpentine shoulders, heavy muzzles, crawling in a patient line.
"T-62s," said Shlomo. "Many."
"'Many' isn't a model," muttered Yitzhak as he hefted the first shell. His hands were fast and calm—like a butcher's, like a midwife's.

"Load HEAT," Avi commanded. "Traverse... left—left—hold—mark. Fire."

The tank shuddered in a way that climbed up your bones and lodged behind your eyes. A breath later, a Syrian turret lifted from its hull as if to test gravity again, then crashed down in a flower of fire. The crew did not cheer. They reloaded.

"Right—two hundred—hold—fire."
Another tank erupted in flame.

The Syrians, shocked by the ferocity of an enemy they had expected unready and dulled by fasting, fanned out, regrouped, pressed harder. The valley—later it would earn a name, a litany of names—gaped like a mouth. Treads wrote black cursive across the hills.

"One o'clock, closing! Range nine hundred!" cried Eyal, his voice pitched high now.
"Fire."
"Hit!"
"Loader!"
"Ready!"
"Traverse!"

The language of battle was always short. The thoughts, never. In the half-seconds between commands, Avi's mind left the periscope and traveled miles. He saw the white light of the synagogue, the Ark open like a chest of gold, his father's lips shaping *Shema Yisrael*. He saw Miriam's hand on Tamar's head, three fingers wide, a small sun in the tendons of her wrist. He saw himself as a boy, peeling an orange on the back steps, the rind coming away in one perfect spiral—ridiculously proud of it. He saw—each vision as sharp as the crosshairs, and gone just as quickly.

A heavy shell struck close, too close, and the tank lifted a foot from the ground before slamming back down. Inside, everything clanged—stainless steel against bone, bone against faith. Smoke coiled in through seams no engineer could seal in time. Yitzhak groaned. "I'm okay," he added a second later, before anyone could ask.

Hours stretched thin. Night did not refresh them. It became a second skin of grit and sweat. The Syrians' green tracer fire drew straight lines of malice; the Israelis' red tracers replied in elegant script. Men died in neat flashes and in ugly ways. On the net, voices rose, broke, vanished. A company commander, whose calm had been ballast for ten men, breathed heavily into the microphone, said, "This is it, boys, I think," laughed then like a fool and said, "Or not," shifted his tanks thirty meters and cut down three T-62s in a row as if dealing cards.

Just before dawn, a shell found Avi's tank.
It did not penetrate—thanks to an angle, a prayer, a mother somewhere still awake with candles—but it slammed so hard against the hull that Avi's definition of "hit" was rewritten. The radio died. The optics turned milky. A fan of shrapnel stitched Yitzhak's thigh. He only noticed when he slid the next round in and left a snail's trail of red across the casing.

"Avi," he said, for the first time with a small voice.

Avi looked down. Time slowed, did that trick where it thickens and you can move through it with your hands. He tore open the first-aid kit, wrapped, knotted; another bandage, another knot—all in the cramped heat that always smelled faintly of metal and old bread. "You stay with me, Yitzhak," he said. "Understood?"
Yitzhak nodded once—the nod of a child told he would not be left behind—and returned to his post at the breech, with the solemnity of a priest returning to the altar.

When the tank finally coughed, shuddered, died, Avi got them out. Night air struck his lungs like a blessing. The tank behind them burned with the private, hungry intelligence of fire; beyond it, the horizon was a row of flickers that marked the edges of hope and danger without distinction.

He dragged Yitzhak to the shadow of a basalt wall. The stones were still warm from the day. He pried a field radio from a dead tank two positions down and growled it to life. "Cohen here, 7th Brigade, northern sector," he said, calmer than he felt. "We're holding. Need ammunition. Need everything."

"Everyone needs everything," came the voice on the net, clipped and dry. "Hold the line."

Avi clicked off and tasted the words. They tasted of iron.

He climbed into a tank whose commander lay folded on the rear deck, eyes open to a sky turning milky gray. "Forgive me," Avi said—because speaking is what keeps us from being only machines—and slid into the turret. He tapped the radio. "Cohen taking over: Twenty-three. Form on me."

Three tanks answered. Then five. Then two more he hadn't counted in his section—drawn like iron filings to a magnet. He heard the men breathe. He heard himself breathe, and the north wind that never seemed to stop once it began.

"Brothers," he said, "there is nowhere to go that is not this place. Behind us lies the Galilee. Behind us our mothers. Behind us Jerusalem. Here we stand."

In the eastern sky the first blade of light broke, thin as a promise and just as sharp.

They held.

Chapter 3 — The Valley Turns

Dawn carved the hills into planes of ash and amber. The Golan awoke to the sound of engines—not birdsong, not prayer, but the stubborn pulse of machines that refused to die. Avi's borrowed tank clattered forward with its small constellation of companions. The air smelled of scorched oil and of a paradox: fear and determination, terror and resolve marching in step together.

"They're massing again," said Eyal, peering toward the horizon. His voice had found its practical register once more—the calm of a craftsman. "Far ridge, line after line—at least two dozen."

Shlomo's jaw tightened. "Range thirteen hundred. We can make them think twice."

"Or make them angry," said Yitzhak, trying a smile that never quite arrived.

Avi made the choice leaders make when perfect options are a myth. "We'll go hull-down on the ridge. Fire on my mark. No wasting shells. Remember—one shot, one truth."

They slid into position like wolves settling against a ridge—just enough metal showing to bite, then retreat. Through the periscope, Avi watched the Syrian line advancing with the confidence of numbers—a long, armored thought. He let them come. He felt his heartbeat slow into the old rhythm of aiming, breathing, deciding.

"Mark," he said.

Shlomo fired. One tank hiccuped flames. Two, three dropped out of line, while red tracers drooled back in reply. The world shrank to a series of windows—periscope, sight, the two-inch strip of sky between mountains—and expanded at the same time into everything behind them: orchards, kitchens, girls doing homework by lamplight, boys pedaling too hard down gravel roads, the thousand small anchors of a land.

A shell ripped earth from the ridge three meters right of the turret. Stones rattled in the commander's hatch like discarded bones. Avi's face did not move. Fear was by now a familiar guest—unwelcome, but not paralyzing.

"Left two degrees. Steady."
"Ready."
"Fire."

Hours lost their edges. Reinforcements came in ragged strands—a company, then a handful of tanks limping in like veterans with walking sticks. Ammunition trucks dashed when they could, halted when they must; their drivers announced life with every gear shift. Across the net, rumors buzzed that the air force had clawed back into the sky, that the first wave had been stabilized, that elsewhere men were doing impossible things without dying of them. You learned to distrust good news the same way you distrusted bad news—slowly, cautiously—until it became truth under your boots either way.

By midday a Syrian tank slipped through a wadi, hunting for a flank shot. Eyal saw it first. "Four o'clock, low. Sly devil."
"Not sly enough," said Shlomo. The gun spoke. The gully blossomed orange; black smoke rolled out like a verdict.

"Count your blessings," Yitzhak muttered.
"I do," said Avi. "Out loud. *Modeh ani* on half a lung."

They laughed, short and absurd—the kind of laugh that bubbles up when the alternative is screaming. Their breath fogged the cramped space and lifted again. The tank hummed, stubborn and loyal as a sewing machine.

By late afternoon, the Syrian wave ebbed, swirled a moment, and broke. The valley that would come to be called *Bik'at HaDema'ot*—the Valley of Tears—hung under the gray haze of spent powder and the animal silence that follows slaughter. Pillars of smoke marked where armor had died. The ridge—that thin, cruel teacher—had once more done its work: rewarding the patient, the precise, the seemingly impossible.

In the lull Avi climbed out and stood on the turret. The wind tasted of copper coins. Far below, ambulance crews moved like meticulous angels among wrecks and men. He saw a medic kneel, place two fingers on a neck, shake his head once, and reach for a blanket. He saw another—not older than Tamar would be in ten years—laugh with relief at a pulse under soot, and then cry as if he had found water in the desert.

Shlomo lifted a canteen. "To home," he said.
Avi drank, letting lukewarm water be a luxury. "To home," he echoed, and in his mind that word was not a place but a covenant: a promise that this hell meant something beyond itself.

The radio crackled alive with a different tone—less desperation, more thread. Orders now had destinations. Lines stiffened. Names of commanders returned to the net; voices of men rumored dead reported positions in clipped syllables. A rear officer, knuckles white on his handset, spoke the sentence that sounded both blessing and challenge: "We held."

Held. Not won—that word would taste sour for some time yet. But: held.

Night crept back, first lavender and then the deep indigo that turns men into shadows. Avi turned the turret once, slowly, like a priest closing a ritual circle, then climbed down. He checked Yitzhak's bandage, now red as a flag. "You're going to a doctor as soon as this becomes 'tomorrow.'"

"If it becomes," Yitzhak agreed, as if time itself were a pendulum the commander could wind.

Avi lay on the glacis, helmet under his head, the tank ticking as it cooled. Above him, Orion drew his belt of stars from its sheath. He thought of the south, of the Sinai, of whispers that the line along the canal had been breached and that people—and nations—were reorienting themselves in jolts, bewildered and furious. He thought of Miriam and Tamar sleeping in a home where the night had learned a new weight. He spoke to the sky as if it had an ear that cared for what he said: "Give me one more dawn," he whispered. "After that, I'll take it from there."

Dawn came.
It did not bring peace. It brought orders.

Chapter 4 — Crossing Water, Counting Names

"South," said the battalion commander, leaning against the hood of a jeep and stabbing at the map with his pencil. "We're rotating armor to the Sinai. The north is holding. The south needs teeth."

The road unfurled beneath them like a reel of film showing another war: dust devils, sudden green oases, the canal glinting like a blade. The Sinai is a land that makes men feel both small and ancient at once; every dune a question, every flat a lie. They passed columns moving in the opposite direction—crumpled tanks from the first days, ambulances grinding down miles, buses full of reservists with pale rings where *tefillin* had been.

At an assembly area west of Refidim the brigade paused to breathe. Fresh ammunition arrived. New orders too: Sharon was probing a crossing—the word on every lip like an impossible rumor—bridges whispered about like contraband. The Egyptians had dug in deep, with missiles that turned the skies into killing fields. But cracks were opening. In war, cracks become doors.

Toward dusk Avi found a quiet spot beside an acacia, its silhouette like an ink sketch. He unscrewed a thermos someone had shoved into his hands and drank coffee that tasted of metal and mercy. He pulled out a small notebook Miriam had tucked into his kit and wrote without following the lines:

Mi she'ana le'Avraham be'Har HaMoria, Hu ya'ane otanu.
He who answered Abraham on Mount Moriah, may He answer us now.

He clicked the pen shut. He did not ask for victory. He asked to be worthy if it came.

The crossing unfolded like something out of a tale old men swear is true. Smoke was laid in curtains. The air force tore holes in the sky and threaded through them. Engineers slid bridges into a river that had believed itself a border, and tanks crawled over them with the careful persistence of beetles. Flares painted the world in theater colors—white, green, blood-orange—and shadows leapt like acrobats.

"Keep it tight," said Avi. "No heroics. The water does not forgive."

On the far bank, Egypt felt different under the treads. The sand was the same, but the angle of history had shifted. They pressed that change in as a shoulder presses open a door. Resistance came—artillery rippling the dunes, anti-tank teams blooming and vanishing like poisonous flowers. The armor rang again; inside, men measured their luck in inches and in whispered *Baruch Hashem*.

They reached an embankment where a lieutenant with sleepless eyes waved them down. "You're the Israelis crossing in daylight?" he asked, as though confirming a rumor about angels.
"Only at night," Avi said dryly. The man barked a laugh he hadn't known he still carried.

Fighting in Egypt tasted different than on the Golan. Distances were longer; the shapes of fear more abstract. Here you learned to read the wind: how smoke lifts and betrays a hidden gun, the seam in a dune that hints at a trench. Here you learned humility before the flats—no ridge to crouch behind, no basalt wall to put your back against while deciding not to die.

By noon they found shelter on the lee side of a low rise, artillery combing the plain ahead like the fingers of a blind giant. Shlomo, who swore he had no use for poetry, stared at the earth and said, "Sand remembers." Nobody mocked him. They all thought of footsteps.

Toward evening a courier arrived with a canvas bag, his motorbike coughing in protest. "Mail," he said, as if the word could exist here. He handed Avi a single envelope, unmistakably in Miriam's round hand.

Beloved, it began. *The whole country still fasts, even those who have eaten. We walk softer, we speak quieter. Tamar asks when you are coming home. I say: when Abba has finished helping the big boys fix something broken. At night I light a candle and whisper your name into it. Come back and argue with me about the leaking sink. I am saving every quarrel.*

Avi read it once, twice. He slipped the letter into his breast pocket with his dog tags, as if the paper could armor the heart beneath it. "Saved quarrels," he said to the crew. "That's home."
"Better than stacked dishes," Yitzhak said.
"Nothing's better than stacked dishes," said Eyal, who had scrubbed his share in the mess tent and knew it.

They pushed forward again, a line of black insects across a white page. They knocked out a rocket battery. They scattered a supply convoy. They saw the map shift color under grease pencil—a slow cheerfulness that felt borrowed, fragile. On the net new words appeared: cease-fire, negotiations. Words that did not belong to tanks—but to tables and pens and the tentative, shapeless courage of men who had tried to kill each other yesterday and were now deciding what to do with tomorrow.

When the cease-fire finally held, it did not arrive like a trumpet blast. It arrived like a man sitting down after standing too long. The guns did not fall silent; they retreated to a distance you could, if you wished, pretend away. Men unclenched their fists. The desert seemed to exhale.

Avi parked the tank and shut off the engine. The sudden silence rang. He climbed down with the stiffness of a much older man and walked until he could see the water he had crossed. It lay there, innocent as ever, blue as a promise.

He pulled out Miriam's letter, read the last line again, and whispered into the wide, patient air: "I am coming home."

Years passed, as they always do—not like a river but like a series of rooms you live in until someone opens a new door. Avi grayed at the temples. Tamar learned long division, then poetry, then the difference between opinion and conviction. The posture of a tank commander softened into that of a father; the sharpness of a commander became the care of a shopkeeper aligning jars neatly on a shelf. He carried a barely noticeable limp. He slept with the hallway light on.

On Yom Kippur he stood each year beside his father—now an old man with a voice like parchment—and whispered the *Shema*. Miriam squeezed his hand at *Ha'melech ha'yoshev*. When the ark opened, Avi's eyes inevitably filled, because memory is a tide that obeys a moon you cannot see.

When he spoke to schoolchildren, he did not tell them he was a hero. He told them of Shlomo's steady hands, of Yitzhak's bandage and stubborn grin, of Eyal's numbers that saved lives. He told them of fear that does not leave and faith that does not either. He told them that courage is not the absence of fear, but the decision that something else matters more.

In his wallet he kept a list of names. Sometimes at night he unfolded it—not because he needed reminding, but because he needed presence. He read them in the same voice with which he had read Miriam's letter in the desert: intimate, reverent, incredulous at the simple fact of each syllable.

One winter afternoon years later he took Tamar, nearly grown, to the monument on the Golan, where basalt is carved with metal and memory. The wind never really stops there. They stood looking out over the valley that had taken and given so much.

"Abba," she said, hooking her arm through his, "what did you learn there that you could not have learned anywhere else?"

Avi considered. The question deserved precision. "That nations are made of very small things," he said. "Not of speeches or maps. Of how someone lays a hand on another's shoulder when the shooting starts. Of how a driver pushes his truck forward inch by inch under fire because he knows what's inside. Of letters. Of quarrels saved for later."

Tamar nodded. The wind swept a loose strand of hair across her mouth; she blew it away and smiled—with a woman's smile now. "And did you learn anything about God?"

Avi looked up at the sky, almost by habit. "Yes," he said. "That He—like the desert, like the Golan—rarely shouts. He waits. And in the waiting, He asks who we intend to be."

They walked back to the car. The road away from the valley curled westward, toward home, toward dinner, toward ordinary mercies. The basalt kept its counsel. The names on the plaques did not fade.

At night, long after Tamar had left for university and Miriam had fallen asleep with a book spread like a tent on her chest, Avi sat at the kitchen table. He wrote a letter to no one in particular and folded it into his wallet beside the list:

We were young and afraid. We fought because the door behind us was the door of our children. The world thought we would break. We did not. We bent. We learned the shape of each other's courage. We crossed water. We counted names. We tried to be worthy.

He turned out the light and stood in the doorway, listening to the house breathe. A small draft slipped in through the window, lifted the curtain, and let it fall again—like a tallit over a sleeping land.

Outside, the land rested—restless, as always, and yet undeniably alive. And somewhere in the north, the valley held fast to its stars.

About the Author

Rabbi Dovied Zwi van der Velde grew up in Holland.

The streets were tidy, the skies often blue—except when the rain came. But Jewish life, at least for him, had to be built almost from scratch in the shadow of the Second World War, when so many Dutch families had lost nearly everyone.

For external reasons, he attended non-Jewish schools his entire life. The local Jewish school was not religious, and so he found himself "the Jewish boy" in classrooms where he quickly learned to keep a little distance, to observe before he spoke. Daily teasing—often followed by beatings—was part of his reality. Yet he never carried his Yiddishkeit quietly. He wore it with stubborn pride: open, visible, unshakable.

Shiurim were scarce. Teachers were rarer still—or at least those willing to deal with a boy both highly intelligent and endlessly energetic. Peers who shared his hunger for Torah were few. At home, his parents—children of a generation that prized responsibility—trained him, lovingly yet firmly, to *"figure it out on your own."* This became his greatest gift. With little structure, he learned to open a sefer and wrestle, to try again when the first door shut, to study in bursts of intensity (what today might be called ADD)—moments of fierce focus followed by stillness.

He finished school early, not because the way was smooth, but because he learned to ride the road he was given—even with all its hidden "silent police" (speed bumps).

He did not walk that road alone. A small inner circle of friends—his age, his equals—accepted him exactly as he was, even when he knew himself to be "a handful." They laughed with him, learned with him, and stayed. *"Thank you for staying anyway,"* he writes, *"you know who you are—and I will love you forever for walking beside me."*

Many Hats, One Heart

Today, Rabbi van der Velde wears many hats but keeps one heart: realtor, insurance broker, rabbi and lifelong learner, husband, father, and grandfather. He is often "there" for those without a table—people who need a place to sit, to eat, to be heard, and to belong.

He serves as a life coach to individuals and families, helping them weave more *shalom*, structure, and *emunah* into everyday life. He leads Home Safe Home Inc. in Lakewood, New Jersey—an effort dedicated to practical *chesed*: providing safety and dignity to people experiencing homelessness; standing with individuals with special needs and their families (see his earlier book *Amazing People*); and creating programs where weekday life and *kedushah* can meet.

He is the designer of a system to better match individuals with special needs, bringing them greater success in building lives and connections. He is also working to establish two ambitious community projects: Special People Village and

Alzheimer's Village—warm, human-centered environments that honor the dignity and daily needs of every soul.

The Voice in This Sefer

From these journeys grew the voice you hear in *Rediscovering Emuna*:

- Gentle, because life taught him how easily a word can wound.
- Practical, because vague inspiration rarely survives Wednesday afternoon.

- Loyal to Chazal, because he needed something unshakable when the ground beneath him shifted.

His writing is for families who want to return to Hashem together—without lectures, ultimatums, or shame. It is for parents and children who long for a table where everyone belongs and no one is turned away.

A Blessing Forward

If this sefer helps you take even a single step—lighting one more candle, speaking one truer word, offering one softer invitation—he asks only that you pass the kindness forward.

May Hashem bless every reader with an open heart, a steady home, and the joy of generations walking together on the road back to Him.